# THE THEOLOGY OF BERNARD LONERGAN

# ÆR

## American Academy of Religion
## Studies in Religion

Editors
Charley Hardwick
James O. Duke

Number 42
# THE THEOLOGY OF BERNARD LONERGAN
by
Hugo A. Meynell

# THE THEOLOGY OF BERNARD LONERGAN

by

Hugo A. Meynell

Scholars Press
Atlanta, Georgia

# THE THEOLOGY OF BERNARD LONERGAN

by
Hugo A. Meynell

© 1986
The American Academy of Religion

**Library of Congress Cataloging in Publication Data**

Meynell, Hugo Anthony.
    The theology of Bernard Lonergan.

    (Studies in religion / American Academy of Religion :
no. 42)
    Bibliography: p.
    1. Lonergan, Bernard J. F.   I. Title.   II. Series:
Studies in religion (American Academy of Religion) ;
no. 42.
BX4705.L7133M493  1987      230'.2'0924      86-3867
ISBN 1-55540-015-9 (alk.paper)
ISBN 1-55540-016-7 (pbk. : alk paper)

Printed in the United States of America
on acid-free paper

For Kai Nielsen
*with much affection and some disagreement*

# CONTENTS

# ACKNOWLEDGEMENTS

A version of chapter 1 was delivered as a talk on the Third Programme of the BBC. Chapters 2, 3, and 4 make use of material published in *The Scottish Journal of Theology, The Heythrop Journal, The Month,* and *Theoria to Theory.* They are published here by kind permission of the BBC, and of the editors of these journals. I am very grateful to Rosanne Sullivan for typing the manuscript, and to Vi Lake for revising it. Last but not least, Professor James Duke has done a great deal to improve the style and overall presentation of the book.

# INTRODUCTION

The main objects of this book are two: (1) To give as clear and simple as possible a view of Lonergan's proposals about theological method, against the background of his theory of knowledge, and to discuss objections made to these proposals; (2) To summarise Lonergan's expositions of the central doctrines of Christianity, in the context of his method. Events have shown that the method is by no means immune to misunderstanding and misrepresentation, and short of some acquaintance with his work on the Trinity and the Incarnation, our view of Lonergan's achievement as a whole is bound to be distorted. The reason why that work is as yet relatively unknown is that it is couched in the decent obscurity of ecclesiastical Latin.

In writing on the history of science, Thomas Kuhn has remarked on the confusion in methods of inquiry and general orientation which prevail in a field before the appearance of a new "paradigm" (Kuhn 1962). Then a mastermind—a Copernicus or a Newton or a Lavoisier—reduces the chaos to order, in such a way that large numbers of problems are solved immediately, and inquirers are set on the road to solving many more. The urgent need for a new "paradigm" in theology would be disputed by virtually no one. If Lonergan has not provided it, as some of us believe that he has, at least his claims to have done so seem worthy of investigation.

It is important to remember that it is one thing to accept the applicability of a method, another to agree to any particular set of conclusions which might be drawn from it. Thus a person might in principle wholeheartedly accept Lonergan's method, and derive Protestant, or Buddhist, or Marxist doctrines from its application. Hence the obvious gap between chapters 1 to 3 on the one hand and chapters 5 to 9 on the other. Chapter 4 attempts briefly to sketch how, in conformity with what Lonergan himself has written, the gap might be bridged. Even granted the premise that Catholicism is true, one may question whether the Latin treatises as they stand are consistent with a thoroughgoing application of the method. Certainly, the treatises were composed before that method had been fully worked out. Nevertheless, I am convinced that there is a fundamental continuity between Lonergan's first-order work in theology and his methodological proposals, and have tried to show that this is so.

Lonergan's writings may be divided into three groups, concerned respectively with methodology (Lonergan 1957, 1972), systematic theology (Lonergan 1964, a, b and c), and the history of ideas (Lonergan 1967, 1971). Owing to the limited aims of this book, very little reference has been made to works in the last category.[1] For similar reasons, I have deliberately refrained from attempting to apply Lonergan's method to the solution of particular problems in contemporary theology. To do so briefly would be a travesty; to do so thoroughly would involve the writing of at least two more books of the same size as this one.[2]

---

[1] The division is not very satisfactory. *Verbum* and *Grace and Freedom* both culminate in systematic theology, when Lonergan makes substantially his own Aquinas' accounts of the Trinity and of divine grace. *Mutatis mutandis,* much the same applies to *Insight.*

[2] For what it is worth, I have tried to do this to a small extent elsewhere, with respect to the doctrine of God in process theology, and contemporary discussions of the Trinity and of the person of Christ. See Meynell 1973, 1976b, 1982, 1983.

# Chapter 1.

# ON THE NATURE OF KNOWLEDGE IN GENERAL

Is theological knowledge possible at all? Can we know, or even reasonably believe, that there is a God, or that there is not a God; or if there is, that God has or has not been revealed in Christ? And if God has been revealed in Christ, what are the sources or authorities on the basis of which we can assure ourselves of exactly what about God has been revealed? Such are the basic questions of Christian theology. According to Lonergan, they can only be properly approached on the basis of an adequate conception of the nature of knowledge in general.[1]

It is a cardinal principle of Lonergan's thought that there are two basic, and contrasting, accounts of knowing, between which there exist various compromises; with these compromises, invariably unsuccessful, the history of philosophy is littered. According to the first of these two accounts, knowing is conceived on the analogy of taking a look. Suppose I am wondering whether my neighbor couple possesses a color television set but do not know whether they do or not. How can I come to know? I can go to visit them and take a look at their set showing a program in color; after that I know what I previously did not know. In this case as in many others, before I take a look, I do not know, and after I have taken a look, I know. Thus the assimilation of knowing to taking a look, or at least the conceiving of it on the analogy of taking a look, is very natural.

But what about my knowledge of your thoughts or feelings, or of events in the past? Plainly, I cannot take a look at what you are thinking or feeling, or at what happened yesterday, let alone a hundred years or more in the past. But, except perhaps on a very restricted account of knowing—about which more will have to be said later—I can all the same come to know such things. For I can at least take a look at *evidence*, in your speech or action or expression, for what you think and feel, or at evidence for what happened in the past, in the formation of rocks for example, or in documents and on monuments. But since the facts which I can come to know in these cases are plainly something over and above the evidence available to my senses for them, it seems to

---

[1] Lonergan's theory of knowledge is worked out and thoroughly applied in Lonergan 1957. For a relatively simple account, see Meynell 1976, in which points made in this chapter are set out and justified at greater length. For brief accounts of his theory of knowledge by Lonergan himself, see Lonergan 1971, chap. 1; and "Cognitional Structures," in Lonergan 1967, 221–39.

follow that there is more to knowing than just taking a look at what is to be looked at, or indeed hearing what is to be heard, or smelling what is to be smelled.

What is the relation, in cases like those which I have just described, between the facts which we come to know and the evidence available to our senses for them? Consideration of this question will bring us to what is, in Lonergan's view, the correct account of what it is to come to know.[2] Basically, one comes to know as a result of putting two sorts of *question*.[3] The first kind of question asks for possible descriptions or explanations of what is available in experience—what may that be? Why may it occur? This kind of question is what Lonergan calls a "question for intelligence." The second kind of question asks, with respect to the answer or answers provided by the question for intelligence, is it so? This is termed by Lonergan a "question for reflection." Evidently it is characteristic of questions of this second kind that they presuppose answers to questions of the first kind, and that, unlike questions of the first kind, they can properly be answered "yes" or "no." I cannot answer "yes" or "no" to a question like "What is the explanation of this?" But if such an explanation is offered (a bull got into the house, the sample was contaminated with barium), I can wonder whether it is probably correct or not. What is that? Perhaps it is a raven. Is it a raven? Taking into account the district, the season, and the poorness of the light, it probably is not, but is more likely to be a carrion crow. Why is smoke rising profusely from the bonnet of the car? The engine is overheating, perhaps. Is it overheating? There is sufficient reason for thinking that it is, and for eliminating other possibilities as much less likely (Lonergan 1957, 82–83, 248, 252, 269–74, et passim).

The examples here given are at once trivial and easy to understand. But the same principles apply to more recondite instances such as those found in the sciences. It is commonplace in contemporary philosophy of science, of course, that to formulate a hypothesis is one thing, to verify or falsify it another. The formulation of a hypothesis is answering the first sort of question, that for intelligence; the verifying or falsifying of it is answering the second, that for reflection. The natural sciences have reached their present highly developed state by repeatedly putting to the data provided by sensation the two sorts of question distinguished by Lonergan. Suppose we have

[2] A superficial objection may be raised against what Lonergan often has to say about "knowing," to the effect that knowing is neither an activity nor a series of activities, as Lonergan implies, but rather a disposition. For example, I do not have to be doing anything, physical or mental, for it to be true at a certain time that I know that five times four is twenty. I merely have to have the disposition to say that it is, when it is appropriate to do so, given that I have insufficient motives for telling lies on the matter; and to act in a manner which is appropriate to its being so. This objection may be countered if, in many contexts where Lonergan speaks of "knowing" (e.g., "Why is doing that knowing?" [Lonergan 1972, 25, 83, et passim]), one speaks rather of "coming to know."

[3] These were first distinguished by Aristotle in the *Posterior Analytics* (II, 2, 89b, 36–38).

before us a pair of rival scientific theories, each providing an account of the same range of data—say, the phlogiston and the oxygen theories of combustion. We have then to determine what the evidence would be which would lead us to reject or retain with good reason each of these theories. Next we establish what the relevant evidence actually is by observation or experiment—at this point we do have to "take a look"—and thereby gain adequate grounds for affirming, at least provisionally, the oxygen theory, and rejecting the phlogiston theory. I say "at least provisionally," since it is conceivable that evidence might come to light in the future which would lead us with good reason to abandon the oxygen theory, as our predecessors did the phlogiston theory.

Now it is of the first importance for Lonergan's account that the entities postulated in a mature science do not correspond directly with what is observed, or even with what could conceivably be observed. "Mass," in Newtonian theory and in contemporary modifications of it, is logically related to force and acceleration (Lonergan 1957, 80, 334–35). It is not exactly the same as the weight you feel when you try to pick an object up, though, to be sure, one can be certain on the whole that the greater the weight of a body, in the sense given, the greater will be its mass. A theory which *accounts for* what is observable is not at all the same as a theory all of whose postulated entities are directly observable. Mass, electrical charge, valency, and the like are notions thought up by scientists in the course of concocting theories; however, although they are not observable, their existence or occurrence is verifiable by appeal to what is observable. The impossibility of taking a look at them does not entail that they are not all the same constituents of the real world, that they are mere "logical constructions" imposed by us in the course of trying to explain the phenomena or to anticipate future developments in some kind of flux of pure sensation (cf., e.g., Russell 1918, 155–57). But there is no temptation to come to such conclusions except on the covert assumption that we cannot know what we cannot take a look at. But if the real world is nothing other than what there is to be known, and if knowledge is a matter of intelligent conception and reasonable affirmation as a result of questions put to experience, we can certainly know what we cannot possibly experience.

Take the tip that knowing is a matter not just of looking or of any kind of experience, but of understanding and judging as a result of questions put to experience, and several famous philosophical problems cease to be problems at all, and a number of persistent methodological errors are eliminated. For example, there is the so-called problem of other minds. How can we come to know the thoughts and feelings of other human beings, when all we can see, hear, or touch is their bodies, the gestures and noises they make, and so on? Behaviorism directly follows from the truth that we can all the same know them, in conjunction with the error that knowing, at least in the proper scientific sense, is really a matter of observing what is known. Behaviorists rightly assert that we can know other people's thoughts and feelings; they also rightly assert that all that we can observe which bears on their thoughts and feelings is their bodily movements and the observable effect of these. But they wrongly conclude that their thoughts and feelings are nothing over and above or other than their bodily movements and the effects of these. It should be obvious that the same mistaken assumptions that lead to behaviorism in psychology lead to "operationalism" in physics—to the view that the theoretical entities postulated by physicists are not really constitutive of the world, but fictions convenient from a practical point of view.

However, on the correct view of knowledge as conceived by Lonergan, where knowledge consists in judgments reasonably made as a result of questions intelligently put to the data of experience, no such conclusions follow. I may think up, by dint of asking "questions for intelligence," a whole range of hypotheses about what you may be thinking or feeling, and then determine, by asking "questions for reflection," which of the hypotheses best fits the evidence provided by your speech and behavior.

If behaviorism is not the proper approach to a scientific psychology, what *is?* According to Lonergan, the proper basic method for achieving an adequate psychological or cognitional theory is to treat one's own mental acts as data, much in the same way as one treats one's sensations as data in the physical sciences. As Gautama, Hume, and others have acutely and quite correctly remarked, I can never actually get a glimpse of myself when I attend to my inner consciousness; I always find a thought, a feeling, or an image, but never myself as such. However, I can, by dint of attending to my acts of observing, questioning, coming to understand, judging, and so on, intelligently conceive that I may be, and reasonably affirm that I am, a conscious subject or self. Once again the principle applies: the fact that I cannot apprehend myself as a datum of outer or inner observation does not entail that I can have no knowledge of myself. The correct metaphysics, or basic account of reality, is for Lonergan the obverse of the correct psychological or cognitional theory. I come to know the real world in reasonable judgments based on intelligent inquiry into a sufficiently wide range of experience. Reality, or the concrete universe, is nothing other than what in principle can thus come to be known (Longergan 1957, xxvii–xxix, chaps. 12–14).

Corresponding to the fully critical account of knowledge and of the real world which knowledge is of, there is an account of what it is to be objective. Reality or the concrete universe, including other persons with their thoughts and feelings, is nothing other than what is to be conceived intelligently and affirmed reasonably on the basis of experience. On this account, the question "How objective are you?" amounts to "How attentive, intelligent, and reasonable are you? Do you envisage a wide rather than a narrow range of possible explanations for the data on any problem? Do you advert to the data on each question? Do you tend to settle for the explanation which best accounts for the data, as opposed to that which soothes your anxieties or gratifies your self-esteem?" Objectivity does *not* merely amount to "How far do you report what is there to be looked at, rather than getting distracted by anything else?" In the human sciences, not only do inquirers aspire to be as attentive, intelligent, and reasonable as possible, but the actions and products of the objects of their study have to be explained as due to a certain mixture of attention and inattention, of intelligence and failure of intelligence, of reason and lack of reason (Lonergan 1957, 562–94).

The conception of objectivity in human science which rules out explanation of human behavior in terms of the "subjective" processes of attention, intelligence, and reason makes it impossible for social scientists to give a satisfactory account of their own work. If, say, one is simply reacting to the chemical processes in one's brain, or to the psychological pressures of one's group, rather than applying one's mind to the evidence with a view to finding out the truth, what reason could there be for taking one's work seriously? This is sometimes forgotten, sometimes rightly admitted to be a serious difficulty, and sometimes shrugged off as philosophical, insoluble, and therefore somehow unimportant.[4] But if the methodological principles of a school of investigators is self-destructive—if it follows from the principles of some psychology or sociology that psychologists and sociologists are incapable of getting at the truth about the matters with which they are professionally concerned—what better reason could there conceivably be for abandoning them? And all theories of knowledge, other than the one outlined, are ultimately self-destructive, according to Lonergan. If their principles are clearly and distinctly conceived, and assented to on the grounds that there is good reason for doing so, then one assents implicitly to the theory of knowledge according to which it is a matter of intelligent conception and reasonable affirmation. If they are not, they are arbitrary, and it is pointless to accept them. On the self-destructiveness of positivism and behaviorism in human studies, the following seems worth quoting:

> How rare is the man that will preface his lectures by repeating his conviction that never did he have even a fleeting experience of intellectual curiosity, of inquiry, of striving and coming to understand, of expressing what he has grasped by understanding. Rare too is the man that begins his contributions to periodical literature by reminding his potential readers that never in his life did he experience anything that might be called critical reflection, that he never paused about the truth or falsity of any statement, that if ever he seemed to exercise his rationality by passing judgment strictly in accord with available evidence, then that must be accounted mere appearance, for he is totally unaware of any such event or even any such tendency. . . . Conscious . . . operations exist, and anyone that cares to deny their existence is merely

---

[4] R. Bierstedt provides a fine example of this maneuvre, in his Introduction to Willer 1972, 2–3.

disqualifying himself as a . . . non-reasonable, non-intelligent somnambulist (Lonergan 1972, 16–17).

As Lonergan sees it, most of the old theories of philosophy, together with the paradoxes too which they give rise, are due either to treating knowledge as though it were taking a look or to one of a series of compromises between this and the fully critical theory of knowledge. The first of the series is the view of John Locke, which still seems to be the dominant assumption in the minds of some physical scientists and many members of the lay public. This adverts to the reason for supposing that the observable properties which we ascribe to things ("secondary qualities") are nothing but the result of their interactions with our sense-organs (are not my visual and aural sensations in my eyes and ears, or perhaps in my brain?), and infers that what really exist are things stripped of these "secondary qualities" (having instead the "primary qualities" of matter in motion).[5] At the next stage of criticism, it is realised that the alleged "primary qualities" supposed to belong to things in the external world are just as much constructions of human intelligence as the "secondary qualities" are dependent on sensation. One may thus conclude, in the manner of Kant or (mutatis mutandis) Bertrand Russell, that the worlds of common sense and science are both of them constructions of thought out of the raw material of sensation. The final stage of this development is represented by Hegel, who recognises that Kant's "things in themselves"—the final shadowy relics of the things of naive realism, which Kant says are unknowable, and yet give rise in some unexplained way to sensation—have no place in a fully critical account of the universe. For Hegel, the common-sense world is a figment of mind or spirit at an elementary stage of development, and the world of science such a construction at a more advanced stage. The world which is somehow prior to, other than, or over and above this, simply does not exist. Hegel's position has been recapitulated in their own terms by contemporary sociologists. Is not our whole conception of "the real world" a social product? And what conception of a world existing over and above our socially-determined conception of the world could we, as social beings, possibly have? (Lonergan 1957, 372–74, 413–16).

In Lonergan's view, Hegel and the social relativists effectively demonstrate the bankruptcy of the naive theory of knowledge, but do not break through to the fully critical account, which gives substance and support both to the common-sense assumption that there exists a world prior to our thoughts about it and to the scientific presupposition that we gain greater and greater knowledge of this extra-mental world. In short, naive realists and empiricists neglect the role of understanding and judgment in our knowl-

---

[5] Lonergan himself cites in this connection not Locke, but Galileo. Cf. Lonergan 1957, 130–32.

edge of the world—verified theories tell us how the world (probably)[6] is, and do not just provide us with convenient means of anticipating future experience. Idealists neglect the role of judgment. It is not the case that the real world either has nothing to do with theoretical constructions which we bring to it, or is actually constructed by us in our theories. The real world is what we come to judge to exist and to be the case in as far as we go on propounding theories and testing them by reference to as wide a range of experience as possible. Thus the world as it really is is simply what we come to know by intelligent and reasonable inquiry into experience. Our "social constructions of reality,"[7] the worlds conceived by different communities, are each the result of more or less attention to data, more or less intelligence in thinking up possible accounts for them, and more or less reasonableness in affirming as certainly or probably true the account for which the data provide sufficient reason (Lonergan 1957, 567). A study of the factors which tend to promote or to militate against the development of attentiveness, intelligence, and reasonableness within communities would constitute the sociology of knowledge, or (perhaps better) of belief such as is widely and confidently maintained.[8]

Renford Bambrough has said in conversation that most of the features supposed to be peculiar to practical reasoning, that is, reasoning about what is to be done, really apply also to theoretical reasoning, or reasoning about what is the case. This reverses a powerful trend in recent philosophy, which has tended to drive a wedge between the latter, as closely controlled by logic and sense-experience, and the former, as committed to an irreducibly arbitrary element of choice. Lonergan's method provides a good illustration of Bambrough's point. Of course, one cannot take a look at the good or the bad, the right or the wrong, as such; thus, on naive realist or empiricist principles, one cannot obtain objective knowledge about them, and one will class moral judgments as expressions of emotion, means of encouraging ourselves and of manipulating other people, and so on.[9] But on Lonergan's account, one comes to know what is good and bad so far as one is attentive, intelligent, and reasonable in determining what will fulfill rather than frustrate the long-term needs and desires of other persons and of oneself.

Yet something more is needed if one is not only to know what is good and right, but to do it. As well as being *attentive, intelligent,* and *reasonable* in

[6] Not, of course, in the sense of the probability calculus. In that sense, as Sir Karl Popper (1972) is quite right to insist, it is the business of a scientific theory to predict events which are highly *im*probable.

[7] Cf. the title of the famous book on the sociology of knowledge, *The Social Construction of Reality* (1967) by Berger and Luckman.

[8] I have heard R. B. Braithwaite make the suggestion that the sociology of knowledge would be better called the sociology of belief.

[9] For "emotivism", see especially Ayer 1958, chap. 6. The classic exposition of "prescriptivism" is Hare 1966.

forming moral judgments, one has to be *responsible* in deciding and acting accordingly. It will be noted that even in purely factual matters more than a little responsibility is involved in committing oneself to find out the truth against all odds, in spite of individual desires and fears and the prejudices of one's group or class. And this is not surprising, since, as most people would instinctively agree, the pursuit of truth is itself an important aspect of the good. And although to be attentive and so on is not itself to be responsible, it is certainly to promote responsibility. Even though you set yourself to find out what is the best thing to do, you may all the same fail to do it. But you will hardly do the right thing unless you exert yourself to find out what it is. And if you intend to do what you know in your heart of hearts is wrong, it is hard to resist restricting your attention, and distorting your intellectual and rational faculties, so that it will appear not to be wrong after all. It is no coincidence, on Lonergan's account of the matter, that moral evil is so often allied with obscurantism; the more irresponsible the classes and individuals, the greater their motives for suppressing attentiveness and inquisitiveness both in themselves and in others (Lonergan 1957, chaps. 6 and 7).

In interpreting, in history, or in the social sciences we use our own experience, understanding, and judgment in coming to know the mixture of experience and lack of experience, understanding and misunderstanding, judgment and failure to judge, decision and refusal to decide, which accounts for the behavior of people in our own society and other societies, in our own historical period and in historical periods other than our own. According to the fully critical theory of knowledge as advanced by Lonergan, a truly objective account of human behavior is one which examines all the relevant sensible evidence, in action, gesture, talk, documents, monuments and so on; which tried to envisage all the possible combinations of experience, understanding, judgments, and decisions by which it might be accounted for; and which judges that the one which best accounts for the available evidence is probably correct (Lonergan 1957, 586–94).

Every society and every group within society has its fund of commonly accepted judgments of fact and value which constitute its common sense. At a comparatively primitive stage, observation and practice will provide criteria for the testing of judgments in a large range of cases, but a capacity for comprehensive criticism is lacking. Thus general and overall accounts of humanity and the world which prevail in such a community are inevitably determined by its members' emotional and imaginative needs. This is the stage of "mythic consciousness," as Lonergan calls it, which does and must prevail before people have the leisure, the inclination, or the intellectual equipment necessary to embark on any comprehensive inquiry into human nature and of the world (Lonergan 1957, 533, 536–42). The next stage begins with that asking of questions about everything for which Socrates was notorious, which in turn springs from the wonder, the disposition to ask questions, which Aristotle claimed was the basis of all science and philosophy.

One begins to speculate, for example, somewhat as follows. These things are what our elders have told us about the nature and doings of the gods. Is what they say really the most satisfactory way of accounting for the evidence we have? Or does it consort better with the view that some interested parties have either been deceived in good faith on these matters or have propagated lies? So begins the process of asking questions, and propounding and testing theories, which has culminated in the mighty achievements of the natural sciences. Through scientific method, and by means of the technical language in which its results are expressed, we move from the common-sense apprehension of things as related to us, closer and closer to knowledge of things as they really are, as related to one another. Some have hoped, so far forlornly, that the same critical process would lead to agreement on the central problems of philosophy. The way to move towards such agreement, in Lonergan's view, is to advert to the human conscious operations of experience, understanding, and judgment which give rise to common-sense and practical knowledge in all communities, and whose thoroughgoing and cumulative employment has issued in the natural sciences. As has already been said, he holds that erroneous positions in philosophy are all ultimately due to mistaking part of the cognitional process for the whole (Lonergan 1957, chap. 17).

In accounting for societies and their institutions, as well as for the words and acts of individual persons, we must take into account not only that people understand, judge, and so on, but that in some circumstances they more or less deliberately avoid understanding. Our wishes and fears may make us unwilling to envisage the possibility that certain things may be so and we are apt to abuse attention, intelligence, and reason accordingly. The effects of this unwillingness in the individual's life have been described by Freud and his followers, whether orthodox or heretical, while Marxists have been particularly concerned with its effects at the political and social level. The relevant sections of Lonergan's work in effect reveal a revised Freudianism, and a revised Marxism, to be particular applications of a comprehensively critical account of individual development and aberration and of social and political progress and decline.

I may become so out of touch with my feelings and desires, by failing to attend to them, and to conceive and judge my mental state accordingly, that the repressed feelings and desires may drastically disturb my conscious living, and I may be driven to seek professional psychiatric help. But the restriction of attention, intelligence, and reason as a result of cowardice or sloth can lead not only to individual neurosis. If we are a powerful group within society, we are liable to have any number of motives for making our group-interest appear identical with the general good of society, and for discrediting or even persecuting those who draw attention to evidence that there may be some discrepancy. As Lonergan sees it, liberals are apt to err by underestimating the human inclination to avoid truth in pursuit of individual and group interest, and Marxists, by misinterpreting its causes and offering cures which may be worse than the disease. Marxists argue—to put the matter in Lonergan's terms—that giving full play to "group bias," with the resulting exacerbation of conflict within society, will lead ultimately to a state of affairs where there is no group-bias and so virtually no conflict at all. According to Lonergan, however, one ought to envisage and work for the general good and in opposition to all group-biases, even those of the most worthy group within society. This view of course presupposes a highly "objective" account of moral reasoning, which, as I have already said, Lonergan maintains can be inferred from his general theory of knowledge (Lonergan 1957, chaps. 6, 7, and 18).

In his later writings, Lonergan has written of "intellectual conversion" and "moral conversion." Intellectual conversion consists in opting for the fully critical theory of knowledge, and applying it to all our opinions, whether common-sense, scientific, philosophical, or religious or anti-religious. This view does not entail the absurd conclusion that we should hold no belief whatever on the authority of others. However, one of the most important functions of intelligence and reason is to adjudicate between competing claimants to authority. Moral conversion consists in envisaging and striving for the objective good, and in setting oneself against all tendencies to individual and group bias both in oneself and one's environment. It is characteristic of group bias to divert attention from inconvenient matters of fact—the realities of factory life as described in Karl Marx's *Capital* do not suit the image that capitalists like to project, or even to express clearly to themselves, of their role in society. Thus, since an adequate cognitional theory shows good and evil to be matters about which one can acquire objective knowledge, and which transcend mere individual option or social convention, it can be seen that intellectual and moral conversion are apt to promote one another. "Religious conversion," which is a matter of being touched and directed by a basic and unconditional love and good will, should give us the heart to put forward the effort and endure the hardship involved in undergoing, and fully implementing, the two other kinds of conversion (Lonergan 1972, 238–43).

Lonergan confirms the instinct of scientists to the effect that, in the theories of physics, chemistry and so on, we transcend the viewpoint of particular places and times, which envisage things as related to us as people of those places and times, and come to know things as they are in themselves, as intelligibly related to one another (Lonergan 1957, chap. II). The point is not, of course, that these sciences as they are at present embody the absolute truth about the matters with which they deal; it is only that they approximate closer and closer to it as more and more observations and experiments are made, and more and more theories propounded and tested.

Is such a viewpoint possible in the study of human beings? According to Lonergan, it is—by the articulation of what he calls "the universal viewpoint" (Lonergan 1957, xxiv, 564–68, 738–39). This involves the clear and distinct realisation, and implementation in the study of societies and of individuals, of the following consideration. Every properly human action or expression is to be understood as the result of some combination of experience or failure of experience; of some understanding or lack of understanding on the basis of that experience; of some judgment on sufficient or insufficient grounds provided by that experience and understanding; and some decision or refusal to decide on the basis of that experience, understanding and judgment. The objection that would spring to the minds of many contemporary philosophers and psychologists, that experience, understanding, judgment and decision are mere 'occult entities,' or at least have no place in an objective science, is to be met by pointing out that it is based on nothing more than the assumption that knowing is a matter of looking, and the mistaken conception of objectivity which results from it. The form of explanation postulated is in fact the very opposite of occult—everybody by the very fact of being human, and *a fortiori* by the very fact of entering into intelligent, reasonable, and responsible discussion with other human beings, is intimately acquainted with the entities which it postulates.

A Lonerganian social science, when it explained an alien society, its institutions, and the actions of its individual members, would neither leave the viewpoint of the society and its members entirely out of account, in the manner of positivism, nor capitulate entirely to that viewpoint, as some would be inclined to do by way of reaction to positivism (e.g., Winch 1958). It would agree with the positivists that an objective and theoretically rigorous social science is possible, while objecting to their conception of how this objectivity and rigor should be conceived and implemented. It would recognise that any agent has some degree of understanding of what he or she is really up to. But, in common with the Marxists, it would point out that this understanding is liable to be restricted and distorted by ignorance and by ideology. The agent's culture may never have reached the stage of theoretical reflection at all, and, whether it has done so or not, individual and group-bias are able to exert their influence. Lonergan would strongly object, however, to the Marxist tendency to sanctify the bias of a particular group or class, even the worthiest. No class is free from a tendency to group bias, however true it is that some classes have more motives for suppressing more of the truth. And one does not have simply to choose between one group-bias and another, given that a moral objectivity based on the universal viewpoint is possible.

In conclusion, "objectivity," in religious matters as elsewhere, is "the fruit of authentic subjectivity" (Lonergan 1972, 292). It is not a matter of putting away one's imaginative capacities and taking a look at reality. Authentic subjectivity consists in attentiveness to experience, intelligence in theorising, reasonableness in judgment, and responsibility in decision. Each of us is conscious of these four operations, and of their more or less thorough exercise, within ourselves. They are not utterly dependent on culture; to the contrary, culture is dependent on them, and progresses or declines in proportion to their exercise. By the rigorous and persistent exercise of the first three, we come to know the world as it really is; by a similar exercise of all four, we come in addition to do what is objectively good. Naive realism and phenomenalism in philosophy are the result of confusing knowing with taking a look; idealism is the result of seeing what is wrong with this, while failing to break through to a fully critical account of knowing. History and the human sciences are a matter of applying experience, intelligence, and reason as rigorously as possible in order to determine the degree of attention to experience, intelligence, reasonableness and responsibility immanent in the actions and products of other people and other societies.

# Chapter 2

## ON THE WAY TO RELIGIOUS KNOWLEDGE

Whether one approves of or deplores the fact, one can hardly deny that among the matters of human interest about which people wish to inquire and gain knowledge are religious matters. Moreover, within human cultures are religious traditions, each of which commends a way of life, along with certain judgments of fact and value supposed to be of very great importance. How are attentive, intelligent, reasonable and responsible persons—authentic human beings—to make up their minds whether to accept the religion of their culture, or to embrace some other religion, or to reject all religion? And how is one to establish exactly what is meant, and exactly what is entailed as a matter of fact or of practice, by any one religion?

A parallel instance may bring the issue into focus. Suppose I am a Marxist theoretician working in Leningrad, trying to clarify and commend the Marxist account of reality and to apply it to the concerns and problems of present-day life. Let us further suppose that I am one of the team employed by the local university for this purpose—Marxism nowadays is a vastly complex and ramifying system of ideas, and one could not reasonably expect any one individual to have a comprehensive and intimate knowledge of Marxism as such.[1] How are we to proceed? The essentials of Marxism are expressed in documents which come to us from the *past*, whether very recent or comparatively remote; and what we have to do is to get at these essentials and to express them in and for the *present*. We may infer that there are two essential phases of our activity, recovering something from the past, and applying it to the present.

In the first phase, we must at the outset become sure (i) that the data are in order—that what we are taking as the basis of our account of Marxism are the authentic writings of (say) Marx, Engels, and Lenin, without spurious additions or corruptions. Having established the best available texts, we then (ii) have to find out what their authors meant by them, as persons of their particular backgrounds in their particular situations. Next, (iii) texts, authors, and meanings have to be fitted into a general objective account of what

---

[1] It is presumably as true for the Marxist as for the Christian or Buddhist that "as time passes, as centers of learning increase, as periodicals multiply and monographs follow one another ever more closely, it becomes increasingly difficult for scholars to keep abreast with the whole movement in their field. For good or ill a division of labor has to be accepted" (Lonergan 1972, 125).

was going forward—this is what the situation was, this is how Marx, Engels, and Lenin responded to it. After this, (iv) value-judgments have to be made: to what extent were they in good or bad faith, to what extent were they correct or incorrect, in doing, saying, or writing as they did? Then we move from the past to the present. We attend first (v) to the intellectually and morally enlightened subject, untrammelled so far as is possible by ideology, who is to assent to the constitutive doctrines of Marxism; then (vi) to the doctrines of Marxism themselves (which the subject who is the topic of (v) arrives at by making value-judgments (iv) about the relevant facts of the past (iii)); next (vii) to a systematic articulation of these which relates them to each other and to the rest of human knowledge and interest, and finally (viii) to making them relevant to every person in every situation.

If we are to relate a traditional way of life and set of beliefs to the concerns of the present, and to be as far as possible clear-sighted and honest about it, each of these steps would seem necessary, and none dispensable. For there must be some kind of available empirical sources, in documents or on monuments, or at least, in some extreme cases, in oral tradition. Those responsible for the sources must have meant something by what they said, did, or wrote (ii), which is bound to be related in some way to what was going forward at that time and place (iii). A value-judgment has to be made, implicitly or explicitly, that what was being expressed by the authors through the sources in the context of what was going forward was more or less right or wrong (iv). A message and a way of life from the past is being commended to right-thinking persons, which presupposes some conception, whether ex- plicit or not, of what a right-thinking person is. (Deliberately to fail to make what is implicit is to be less than honest; covertly to appeal to a subject's hatred or aggressiveness or self-esteem usually has a very different effect from making it clear that one is doing so. The importance of stages (iv) and (v) is largely that they bring this kind of issue to light.) If the message and the way of life amount to anything at all, they can be expressed in a series of judgments of fact and value (vi). If they are coherent and of general applica- tion, this coherence and general applicability can be brought out (vii), and the application made to each particular case (viii).

How are these considerations to be applied to religion? Christianity and other religions involve applying a message given in the past to human living in the present and future. In reflecting on the nature of a religion, two basic things are to be done: to recover the message; and to state it and apply it in the present. The two phases of theology thus to be distinguished, Lonergan labels *mediating* and *mediated* (Lonergan 1972, 135). The Christian message (to take the example employed by Lonergan himself)[2] comes to us through a community which, over the course of the centuries, has expressed its witness

---

[2] It is *not* the case, in spite of what has sometimes been claimed, that Lonergan in *Method* moves directly and without justification from setting-out general methodological considerations to assuming the truth of Roman Catholic Christianity. See chap. 3 below.

to Christ in a number of documents. We have then (i) to establish what is the actual content of the documents, (ii) to understand what the authors of the documents meant in writing as they did, and (iii) to relate authors and documents in a coherent narrative along with the other persons, events and circumstances of their times. Here then we have the first three of the "functional specialties" into which Lonergan divides theology: *research, interpretation,* and *history.* So far we are in the realm merely of what we may call "religious studies;" we have adverted only to what those within the religious tradition said and meant and the circumstances in which they said and meant it, and not to the question of to what extent and in what respects they were justified in saying and meaning what they did. This question is taken up in the fourth functional specialty, *dialectic,* in which one moves from accurate description of the past to evaluation of it, from history in the manner of Ranke to history in the manner of Burkhardt.[3]

With the fifth functional specialty we shift to the second phase. *Foundations* explores the nature of human authenticity or conversion in the three dimensions distinguished by Lonergan, intellectual, moral and religious. *Doctrines* sets out clearly and distinctly the judgments of fact and value to be assented to by the converted subject in the religious tradition concerned. The seventh functional specialty, *systematics,* aims at achieving an understanding of the doctrines, a conception of how they all cohere and how they relate to the rest of human knowledge and opinion. In the eighth and last functional specialty, *communications,* the body of doctrines understood in systematics is brought home to all human persons in their particular circumstances, and at their particular stage of intellectual development. Thus the whole process of bringing the Christian message to bear on present circumstances is completed, with each specialty playing its necessary and indispensable role in the process (Lonergan 1972, chap. 5).

### *Chart of the Functional Specialties*

| First Phase: Mediating | Second Phase: Mediated |
|---|---|
| 1. Research | 5. Foundations |
| 2. Interpretation | 6. Doctrines |
| 3. History | 7. Systematics |
| 4. Dialectic | 8. Communications |

Functional specialties are to be distinguished from the more familiar field specialties. The trouble with the division of theology according to field specialties—Old Testament, New Testament, Patristics, Medieval, and so

---

[3] I shall use such terms as "research" and "history" in italics when referring to the functional specialties, to avoid confusion with their normal senses.

on, with all the subdivisions of each—is that theologians tend to come to know more and more about less and less, and in proportion as they do so exaggerate the significance of their particular study for the business of theology as a whole (Lonergan 1972, 137). It is no coincidence that the eight functional specialties correspond closely to the four basic conscious opera-tions distinguished in the first chapter. Human conscious activity consists basically of experience of data, understanding, judgment, and decision. The functional specialties of the first phase respectively make available the data, understand them, judge what was going on, and make a decision with respect to it; those of the second phase articulate present decision, set out the judgments in terms of which it is expressed, come to an understanding of the systematic interrelation of the judgments, and in implementing this understanding in the activity of contemporary life give rise to a new set of data. One will not deny, of course, the obvious fact that every basic type of conscious activity is involved in each of the functional specialties.[4] To do *research*, for example, one has to be attentive, intelligent, reasonable, and responsible rather than merely attentive; and the same applies *mutatis mutandis* to the other functional specialties (Lonergan 1972, 133–34).

One may ask how one may establish in the first place what are the relevant texts. As Lonergan points out, the functional specialties do not simply depend upon one another in numerical order from one to eight. In establishing what the appropriate data are (is it to be the Bible, the Koran, or the Vedas?), *dialectic, foundations,* and *doctrines* would all be relevant. That the Koran is the source *par excellence* for the revelation of God, in a way and to a degree that the Bible is not (for example), would itself be a *doctrine,* to be affirmed or denied by an authentic subjects (the topic of *foundations*) who had evaluated (on the basis of *dialectic*) what was said each in terms of their own historical milieu by the relevant authorities.[5]

Before dealing with the functional specialties in greater detail, some of the more important notions that Lonergan employs in *Method in Theology* must be briefly introduced. As was said a little earlier, he distinguishes three types of conversion constitutive of human authenticity, intellectual, moral and religious. To reject all traces of the cognitional myth of naive realism, which assimilates knowing to taking a look—to cast out its pervasive and pernicious leaven from the lump of our thinking—is what Lonergan calls intellectual conversion. Intellectual conversion will tend to lead to con-version of the two other kinds when consistently followed through. Moral conversion may be summarised as the shift of our endeavors from the realisation of satisfactions to that of values. To crave sleep or food or sexual activity is one thing; to envisage and to work for a state of society within

---

[4] For misunderstanding on this point, see chap. 3 below.

[5] Lonergan speaks in terms of a Christian rather than a fully ecumenical context here, but it is easy to apply what he says more broadly.

which such wants, needs, and desires in oneself and others may be met, is another. The crucial distinction is between the good as directly needed or desired on the one hand; and on the other hand the good as object of experience, understanding, and judgment of how the desires and needs of sentient beings in general may be satisfied. Religious conversion is submission to an otherworldly love which is such as to undergird and intensify the other types of conversion and to hearten us to implement them fully and consistently in the face of discouragement (Lonergan 1972, 238–44).

*Insight* demonstrates how intellectual conversion, when followed through, leads first to moral and then to religious conversion (Lonergan 1957, esp. chaps. 18 and 19). But Lonergan admits that the three conversions generally occur in the reverse direction. One first responds, whether one is fully conscious of the fact or not, to God's offer of love, and then is led to put one's moral, and perhaps ultimately one's intellectual, house in order. The relationship between intellectual and religious conversion implies that arguments for the existence of God do not usually bring about religious conversion, though they do have a secondary role to play. Before an argument makes sense, one has to be within the intellectual horizon within which it makes sense, and for a person to have reached this intellectual horizon by anything approaching a thorough and accurate account of the nature of human knowing is rather rare (Lonergan 1972, 338–40).

It will be universally agreed that a distinction has to be made between the ordinary language concerned with everyday things and interests and the technical languages typical of the sciences. It is not implausible to suggest that in order to grasp the difference between these two types of discourse, one must give attention to the inquiring human subject who is the source of both. Such an inquiry into the inquiring human subject is at the basis of Lonergan's distinction between different realms of meaning. The realm of common sense regards the things and activities of everyday living; it is never transcended at all by a large proportion of humankind. The realm of theory, discovered by the ancient Greeks (Lonergan 1972, 91–92), derives from a sustained putting of questions about these things and activities—the natural sciences and Scholastic theology, with their technical languages, belong to this realm. It aspires to a description and explanation of things as they really are in themselves, rather than as related to us, to our interests and our sensory capacities (Lonergan 1957, 79–82). The medieval attempt to recast Christian theology in Aristotelian terms was essentially an application of the realm of theory to what was expressed in a more direct and concrete manner in the language of the Bible (Lonergan 1972, 309).

Another realm of meaning, the scholarly, was first entered by the German historical school of the nineteenth century. Scholarship enables one to understand the common sense of people at a time and place widely different from one's own. The realm of interiority, which is explored by Lonergan's book *Insight* and by contemporary phenomenological philosophers, regards the conscious human subject whose mental operations give rise both to the realm of common sense and to those of theory and of scholarship, and makes their viewpoints reconcilable. To take a notorious example, Pascal's distinction between the God of Abraham, Isaac, and Jacob on the one hand, and the God of the philosophers, on the other, is not really a distinction between two putative Gods, but between the one God as envisaged respectively from the viewpoint of common sense and from the viewpoint of theory.[6] To enter any realm of meaning other than that of common sense, one needs to acquire the corresponding "differentiation of consciousness."[7]

An investigation of the realm of interiority is what makes possible transcendental method, that is, inquiry into inquiry as such. One investigates what it is to be attentive, intelligent, reasonable, and responsible, and applies the moral in a way that is relevant to the particular subject in which one is interested. Such a method encounters head-on the difficulty which is perhaps above all the source of the present crisis in theology. This is, that whereas culture once appeared to be single and normative (one acquired it by means of a classical education), we now know that there are many different cultures. This realization poses special problems for the expression of a faith which is to be preached to all nations, but each of whose doctrines is expressed in terms whose meanings are defined within particular cultures at particular stages of development. But the trans-cultural base needed to determine identity in meaning between doctrines formulated in various cultures at various stages of development is in fact provided by transcendental method, which works on the sole assumption that all persons at all stages of civilisation may be more or less attentive, intelligent, reasonable, and responsible.[8] The assumption that there is just one culture, and the insistence on uniformity of expression which generally goes with it, is what Lonergan describes and deplores as "classicism" (Lonergan 1972, 124, 302, 326, 363).

At first sight one may find it annoying that Lonergan attributes the so-called "fideism"[9] of Karl Barth, Rudolf Bultmann's assertion of the irrelevance of historical investigation to faith, and the hostility of prominent scientists towards Christianity to absence of "intellectual conversion" (Lonergan 1972, 318). A sceptic may be forgiven for concluding that "intel-

---

[6] On the role of philosophy within theology, see Lonergan 1972, 337–38.

[7] On "differentiations of consciousness," see *Method*, 258–62, 302–18.

[8] On the transcultural significance of transcendental method, see Lonergan 1972, 17.

[9] It may be objected that Barth is not a "fideist" in precisely the sense of the term in which "Fideism" was condemned by the First Vatican Council. However, what Lonergan seems to mean by fideism is rejection of the view that human intelligence and reason working independent of divine revelation can in principle find valid grounds for asserting the existence of God. In this sense, Barth would appear to be a fideist, both in his general attitude to what he calls "natural theology" and in his well-known insistence that belief cannot argue with unbelief, only preach to it. I am grateful to T. F. Torrance for raising this objection in conversation.

lectual conversion" is just a sententious and misleading expression for agreement with Lonergan. But this would be a superficial view. Everyone would
agree that one cannot conceivably take a look at God. Thus, if knowing in the
ordinary senses is fundamentally a matter of taking a look, then either the
atheist is right that one can know that God does not exist, or God must be
"known" in a way which has nothing to do with anything else which goes by
the name of knowledge. But Lonergan argues, for reasons sketched in the
last chapter, that this account of knowledge is mistaken. The correct account,
when worked out and followed through, is not inimical to belief in God, and
not even neutral towards it. It actually tends towards it when its full implications are realised, and once it has been purged of contamination by the
erroneous conception of knowledge just mentioned. To put it briefly and
crudely, science when properly understood leads not to matter in motion as
the term of explanation, but to an intelligible order ultimately to be accounted for only as due to the activity of a creative intelligence (Lonergan
1957, chap. 19; Lonergan 1972, 101).

A number of illustrations may be given of the need to distinguish the
functional specialties sharply from one another, if theology is to be done with
rigor and honesty, and not to be vitiated by ideology (Lonergan 1972, 357).
Obviously to tell an edifying story about the origins or the activities of one's
religious group is one thing; to set out the facts as they really were is another.
That is to say, the aims of the eighth functional specialty *(communications)*
are different from those of the third *(history)*; and while *communications* may
properly take advantage of the deliverances of *history*, to allow it to affect the
actual business of doing *history* is the royal road to imposture and fraud. For
example, Cranmer's actions at the stake, it appears to me, really were
edifying, but the question of what he did and said must be decided without
reference to edification, but simply by examination of the evidence. Again,
technical and abstruse language is needed both to express doctrines clearly
and distinctly (the sixth functional specialty) and to understand how they
cohere into an intelligible unity (the seventh). But to expound the doctrines
thus clearly expressed and understood to the person in the pew, a different
style and manner are needed. The person in the pew probably cannot
understand just what it is for Christ to be consubstantial with the Father, but
if one is an orthodox Christian one will have a degree of devotion to Christ
which would be blasphemous if he were not. To reproach *doctrines* and
*systematics* for not being *communications*, as is in effect so often done, is like
reproaching cancer-research for not applying itself directly to the cure of
patients. The former task, while not identical with the latter, is a necessary
condition of its being done properly. I think it is the vice of much recent
theology seriously to neglect the fourth, fifth, sixth, and seventh functional
specialties. However well instructed the clergy may be in *research, interpretation,* or religious *history,* they cannot apply their knowledge directly to

preaching without the intervening disciplines which deal with the determination of the essentials of the faith and their transposition from the varying contexts of the past to that of the present.

It is the special province of the sixth functional specialty to determine the element of permanence in religious doctrine in relation to change. This task has become an acute problem in recent times, when historical studies have made thinking people vividly aware of the profound differences between our own worldview and the worldviews of earlier Christian generations. What sense does it make, one may ask, to maintain that we continue to hold the same faith that they did? As Lonergan sees it, the witness of the Church is "to the mysteries revealed by God and, for Catholics, infallibly declared by the Church. The meaning of such declarations lies beyond the vicissitudes of human historical process. But the contexts, within which such meaning is grasped, and so the manner, in which such meaning is expressed, vary both with cultural differences and with the measure in which human consciousness is differentiated" (Lonergan 1972, 327).

Reflection on the New Testament made the early Christian Fathers wonder whether and in what sense Christ could be truly man and truly God, and having decided that he really was one individual at once human and divine—in technical terms, that he was one "person" in two "natures"—they were well embarked on that theoretical re-casting of the Biblical witness which was to find its full development in medieval scholasticism. But in addition to the realm of common sense and that of theory, there is the realm of interiority. According to Lonergan, if we are to do for our age what the great scholastics did for theirs, we must transpose their theory into categories derived from that realm (Lonergan 1972, 327–28). Someone might object that the attempt to reconcile permanence with change in doctrine is a mere verbal quibble, but a parallel with mathematics shows that this need not be so. That two plus two equals four is grasped in one way by an ancient Babylonian, in another way by an ancient Greek, in yet another by a modern mathematician. Yet it is the same truth, that two plus two equals four, that is grasped by all of them in their different ways (Lonergan 1972, 325).

Religious doctrines are proclaimed at first in terms of a particular culture and a certain differentiation of consciousness. Later, they are proclaimed to other cultures and to persons whose consciousness is otherwise differentiated. For this to happen, it is necessary that the doctrines be recast. (It is useless to tell a Greek or a Roman, or *a fortiori* a Zulu, that the Messiah has come, since "messiah" is a term whose meaning is bound up with a particular historical environment which is foreign to them.) The necessity for such recasting, as we shall see, provides an explanation in general terms both of what has happened to date in the development of Christian doctrine, and what remains for theologians to do.

On Lonergan's account, a number of stages are to be distinguished in the human mind's discovery of itself. (i) Each of us spontaneously lives and thinks in terms of the common sense characteristic of our place and time; for most of human history, no one got beyond this stage, and most people up to the present have remained in it. (ii) God's gift of love provides for human living an orientation which may be manifested in any number of ways and rejected in as many more—as is illustrated by the glories and monstrosities of each religious tradition. (iii) Human knowing and feeling being incomplete without expression, literature and the arts develop. (iv) Systematic meaning begins to develop when, like Socrates, one starts looking for definitions (Lonergan 1974, 252). By doing so, and by coining terms to express the definitions and defining their interrelations, one comes up with an explanatory and well-ordered view of this or that realm of experience. (v) In post-systematic literature, educated classes within a society express their acceptance of the systematically-grounded critique of earlier common sense, literature, and religion, without themselves being systematic thinkers. Their thinking is generally in the common-sense mode, even though they may on occasion make use of a technical term or a logical technique. (vi) With the development of scholarship, one aspires to understand the common sense of places and times other than one's own; this is the sort of goal aimed at by exegetes and historians. (vii) When scholarship has established itself, there arises a post-scientific and post-scholarly sort of literature which stands to science and scholarship much as post-systematic literature did to ancient system. (The vast majority of articulate modern writings of a non-technical nature belong to this category.) Finally, (viii) the exploration of interiority, by which one comes to identify in one's own experience one's conscious acts and their interrelations with one another, provides both an invariant basis for systems changing over time, and a point of view from which one can explore all the differentiations of human consciousness (Lonergan 1972, 303–5).

This last point needs expansion. The gist is that in becoming fully conscious of my own processes of thought, I can get the hang of how human thinking may become specialised in all the ways of which it is capable. I can come to a clear grasp of just what it is to have experience, to understand, to judge, and to decide. From this vantage-point, I can come to realize what it is to go on asking questions on a topic until I gain a coherent and logically consistent view of it, as in the empirical sciences and in scholastic theology. I can also apprehend what it is, in the scholarly mode of thought, to read documents and decipher monuments until I am able to grasp how the persons of a place and time other than my own felt, understood things, made judgments and decisions, spoke and acted—and so on.

How does all this apply to the reflection on religion which is the essence of theology? To take the Christian case as an example, the Bible presupposes stages (i), (ii) and (iii)—common-sense apprehension of the world, God's gift of love, and literary and artistic expression. But the authors' viewpoint was pre-systematic and pre-scholarly. However, even from this point of view, one may reject the false and approximate to the true. The Old Testament writers, it appears, used the traditions of neighboring peoples to provide means for the expression of something quite different.

> The God of Israel played his role in a very real human history. Questions about creation and the last day were concerns with the beginning and the end of the story. There was no mention of a primeval battle of the gods, or a divine begetting either of kings or of an elected people, no cult of the stars or of human sexuality, no sacralising of the fruitfulness of nature (Lonergan 1972, 306–7).

Similarly, we find in the New Testament a symbolism also found in late Judaism and Hellenistic Gnosticism, but always used in subordination to specifically Christian purposes. (What are "specifically Christian purposes" may be found by applying the first six functional specialties to the whole past Christian tradition.) A slight tincture of systematic meaning begins to appear in the Greek councils from Nicea onwards—a logical technique was employed, such as is available to those who live in an environment influenced by post-systematic literature (the fifth stage in the mind's discovery of itself mentioned above), and involves reflection on propositions rather than directly on things. Neglect of this move towards systematic meaning is what gives rise to the common objection to the Greek councils, that they imported alien "Greek" notions in exposition of the essentially "Hebraic" content of Christian faith (Lonergan 1974, 22–27).

The original use of the term "consubstantial," although often treated as though it were impenetrably obscure, becomes luminously clear when one bears the point in mind that it directly regards propositions about things rather than things themselves. As Athanasius explained it, it "is not some speculative flight concerned with an apprehension of the divine being or essence. It quite simply means that what is true of the Father also is true of the Son, except that the Son is not the Father" (Lonergan 1971, 306–7). Once the move towards system, towards the presentation of the faith as a logically coherent whole, had begun, it could not be stopped. Soon the question had to be settled of whether the Holy Spirit in addition to the Son is consubstantial with the Father (Constantinople I). Next, it had to be determined whether it is really the case that one and the same was born of the Father before all ages and born of the Virgin Mary in the reign of Augustus Caesar (Ephesus). Ultimately, it had to be stated that one and the same could be both temporal and eternal, mortal and immortal, because he had two natures, a human and a divine (Chalcedon) (Lonergan 1972, 313). It is again to be emphasised that the use of the terms "person" and "nature" in the decree of Chalcedon is basically a very simple matter, whatever later speculation may have made of it. "Chalcedon mentions person and nature because it is aware that people may ask whether divinity and humanity are one and the same and, if not, how it is that the Son our Lord Jesus Christ is one and the same. The Son our Lord is one person, divinity and humanity are two natures" (Lonergan 1972, 308).

In the Middle Ages, Lonergan maintains, a thorough effort was made to recast the faith in systematic terms; more and more terms were precisely defined, and more and more problems solved. For example, Peter Lombard fixed a precise meaning for the ancient and ambiguous term "sacrament," and then found that there were seven sacraments in the Church. Again, the Middle Ages had inherited Augustine's affirmation of both divine grace and human liberty. After much agonising over the matter in the twelfth century, when attempts to articulate the relation seemed always to destroy either grace or liberty, a method was hit on in the thirteenth century of discussing liberty without bringing in grace, and discussing grace without bringing in liberty, and so of working out the relation of the one to the other.[10] All this effort amounted to an attempt to recast the faith in systematic terms (in accordance with stage (iv) above). To achieve this transformation, and to provide the overall conceptual framework for it, theologians at the time could hardly have done better than to adopt and adapt the work of Aristotle (Lonergan 1972, 310).

However, it is evident that Aristotle has now been superseded; Lonergan notes that although Aristotle magnificently represents the emergence of system, he does not envisage either the scholarly differentiation of consciousness or the succession of systems taken into account by a fully articulate method. Aristotelian system claims to deal with what is necessarily so; the systems of modern science are only verified probabilities, subject to revision when a system is found which more adequately accounts for the relevant data. To do for our age what the greater scholastics did for theirs, we must find in interiority the basis for both the common-sense and the systematic differentiation of consciousness, and hence come to understand the identity of the one faith in Jesus Christ through all the changes due to variations in culture and in differentiation of consciousness.

A crucial factor here is the historical sense which is the fruit of the scholarly differentiation of consciousness; without it, anachronism or archaism is inevitable. "The anachronist attributed to Scripture and to the Fathers an implicit grasp of what the Scholastics discovered. The archaist, on the other hand, regarded as a corruption any doctrine that was not to be found in the plain meaning either of Scripture or of Scripture and the patristic tradition" (Lonergan 1972, 312). We have to grasp in terms of interiority, scholarship, theory, and the common sense of our own particular place and time, the faith that the Bible presents in terms of Hebrew and Hellenistic common sense, the medievals in terms of theory. Because there are so many points of view from which the one faith in Jesus Christ may be grasped, a plurality of doctrines, rather than a single set of formulae demanding every-

---

[10] For the history of this development, see Lonergan 1971, 13–19.

one's assent will be necessary. Method based on interiority will show where differences in expression are benign, due to differences in culture and differentiation of consciousness, and where they are more serious, due to lack of intellectual, moral, or religious conversion. Benign differences testify to the vitality of faith, since one's grasp of it, if deep and genuine, will be expressed in the terms and conceptions proper to one's own culture (Lonergan 1972, 326–30).

While *doctrines* aims at a clear and distinct affirmation of religious realities, *systematics* aims at understanding these realities. Systematic theologians endeavor to show *how* those things are so which their religion proclaims *are* so. "It wants its understanding to be true, for it is not a pursuit of misunderstanding. At the same time, it is fully aware that its understanding is bound to be imperfect, merely analogous, commonly no more than probable." After all, it would be blasphemous, or ridiculous, to expect an exhaustive understanding of the mystery which is God. And in any case the explanations of the systematic theologian, like those of the empirical scientist, are only provisional hypotheses open to correction. The assent to doctrines is the assent of faith, which is commonly regarded by religious persons as firmer than any other. However, the *understanding* accompanying such assent has traditionally been regarded as very variable. From very early in its history, the Christian Church acknowledged that although one believer might be far more articulate than another, this did not imply that the latter was less a believer (Lonergan 1972, 349–50).[11]

Systematic theology often has to face the charges of being "speculative, irreligious, fruitless, élitist, irrelevant." Speculative it can be and has been. But Lonergan insists that, as he conceives it, it is, in principle at least, quite a homely affair, aiming merely at an understanding of the truths of faith. It may become irreligious, as is particularly liable to happen when its main emphasis is on proof rather than conversion, or when a person takes up a position or maintains it out of individual or group pride. It has its fruitless aspects as well, since misunderstanding as well as understanding can be systematised. But one is not at the mercy of such misunderstanding when one adverts to it, and sets up criteria for distinguishing between positions which are due to the presence of intellectual, moral, and religious conversion, and "counter-positions" which are due to their absence (Lonergan 1972, 350). It *is* élitist, but this it has in common with mathematics, science, scholarship, and philosophy, since like them it is difficult, in application if not in principle. "But the difficulty is worth meeting. If one does not attain, on the level of one's age, an understanding of the religious realities in which one believes, one will simply be at the mercy of the psychologists, the sociologists, the philosophers, that will not hesitate to tell believers what it really is in which they believe." Systematic theology, finally, will be irrelevant unless it issues in communications. But it is absolutely necessary for

[11] Lonergan cites Irenaeus, *Adv. Haer.*, I, 10, 3.

effective communications, since in order to communicate anything effectively one must understand what it is that one is trying to communicate (Lonergan 1972, 351). And it is worth pointing out that the clarity, conciseness, and organisation of Catholic doctrines from medieval times up to the Second Vatian Council have been due to the use of conceptions and terms originally worked out by systematic theologians (Lonergan 1972, 311–12).

To clarify further what *dialectic* involves, we must say something about Lonergan's conception of a "horizon." A horizon is literally, of course, the limit of a person's field of vision. The metaphorical use of the term at issue here derives from the fact that just as our range of vision is bounded, so is that of our knowledge and interests. Differences of horizon are often related as stages within a single process of development or, in a complementary manner, like those characteristic of different skills or professions which recognise one another's expertise (as a doctor and a lawyer, or a physicist and a palaeontologist, might do). But differences of horizon are of concern to *dialectic*, in the sense intended by Lonergan, only when what is reckoned true, intelligible, or good within one horizon is reckoned false, unintelligible, or evil within the other. In such cases the one horizon, or some part of it, seems from the other to be due to ignorance, or wickedness, or refusal of God's grace, or whatever. A person's horizon is the result of past achievement or failure; it at once makes possible one's further development, and sets limits to it. What does not fit into one's horizon tends to be overlooked, and when forced on one's attention, to be dismissed as irrelevant and unimportant. Each of the three types of conversion involves a change of horizon, such that the adoption of the new entails a repudiation of characteristic features of the old (Lonergan 1972, 235–38).

The basic maxim of *dialectic* is to "develop positions" and "reverse counter-positions" in the material being studied—that is, to follow out the implications of statements compatible with the three types of conversion and to repudiate the statements incompatible with them along with their consequences. This work will of course be performed very differently by investigators in different horizons. But the source of the lack of uniformity will appear when investigators clearly distinguish between what they would regard as "positions" and what they would regard as "counter-positions," and indicate what they think would result from developing the former and reversing the latter. And the process is taken still further when the results achieved thus far are themselves taken as materials for the exercise of *dialectic* (Lonergan 1972, 249–50). The ultimate goal of *dialectic* is a comprehensive viewpoint from which every human horizon can be explained in its virtues and deficiencies, in a manner analogous to what is sought for and largely found with regard to the material world by the natural sciences.[12]

Theologians should be second to none in setting out to know what is true

12 For Lonergan's notion of the "universal viewpoint," see p. 17 above.

and what is good, against all prejudice or bias arising from their own circumstances and the groups of which they are members. Only in this way can one become fit to discern the ambivalence at work in others and in the way they resolved their conflicts. Only in this way can one properly appreciate the intelligent, the true, and the good in the life and thought of one's opponents; and the misinformed, mistaken, and evil in those of one's allies. Lonergan stresses that it is our own self-knowledge which enables us to know others accurately and to judge them fairly. Conversely, knowledge and appreciation of others helps us to know ourselves and to refine our apprehension of values. In the process of pronouncing on positions and "counterpositions," and developing the one and reversing the other, we reveal ourselves. We are liable then, if we are open-minded and sincere, to ask some basic questions, first no doubt about others, but ultimately about ourselves. Results are unlikely to be immediate, since conversion is usually a slow process of maturation. "It is finding out for oneself and in oneself what it is to be intelligent, to be reasonable, to be responsible, to love." *Dialectic* promotes this discovery by drawing attention to basic differences, and to the example of others who differ radically from oneself. We are thus invited to a self-scrutiny, which perhaps ultimately leads to a new understanding of ourselves and our destiny. Indeed, one may say of this method as a whole that its "basic idea takes its stand on discovering what human authenticity is and showing how to appeal to it" (Lonergan 1972, 252–54).

In approaching any text, whether by friend or foe, from the point of view of *dialectic*, the investigator is faced with the following sorts of question. How intelligent, reasonable, responsible, and in love with God does it reveal its author to be? How far, on the contrary, does it bring out that one was biased because of one's individual circumstances or one's membership in a group or class? On the other hand, to what extent does its content unsettle one by revealing lapses in one's own authenticity, by showing up biases of one's own? Is one tempted to repudiate it, belittle it, or shrug it off because of this? Lonergan does well to emphasise the role of "resentment," of what one feels more or less obscurely to be intellectually, morally, or spiritually superior to oneself, as a motive force in human speech and behaviour (Lonergan 1972, 33, 273).[13] One could wish that awareness of its prevalence were more characteristic of academicians.

Suppose I am annoyed by Marx or one of his followers when they are writing about religion. If I disagree with what they say, how far is this due to the group-bias of my class, rather than to the reasons which I profess? As an academician in the western world, I may well wonder to what extent I am really in the business of fostering the inattention to evidence, the refusal to ask pertinent questions, and the moral renunciation which go with my

---

[13] Lonergan takes this notion from Max Scheler, who in turn derived it from Friedrich Nietzsche.

privileges and with those of the persons who secure my livelihood. Again, if I find the Latin Fathers offensive when I read them on sexual morality, to what extent is this a matter of reasonable judgment of mine about the hang-ups they had due to psychological ignorance or quasi-Manichean devaluation of the body; and to what extent is it because I want to excuse my own sexual weaknesses, and the lack in love of God of which they are a symptom, by belittling them? We all make snap value-judgments and decisions about such matters without sufficiently adverting to what we are up to and it is not the least of the merits of Lonergan's method that it brings this process to the center of attention, deliberately shedding light on matters which in most academic discussions are kept in darkness.

In *foundations*, there is articulated the extra element which is required "to move from the indirect discourse that sets forth the convictions and opinions of others to the direct discourse that states what is so" (Lonergan 1972, 267). This extra element can only be human authenticity—the person attentive, intelligent, reasonable, responsible, and loving; any other basis for objectivity than such authentic subjectivity, perhaps some more subtle version than ever of what is there to be looked at, is just delusion (Lonergan 1971, 292). The foundational reality, which is conversion, is a matter of discovering what is inauthentic in oneself and turning away from it; it is thus very relevant to the Christian gospel, which summons people to repentance (Lonergan 1972, 270). In doing theology, of course, the subject does not operate in a vacuum; there is the accumulated wisdom of one's religious tradition to which one has to attend (Lonergan 1972, 289). The great religious traditions interpret religious experience very differently; Christians interpret it as the love of God flooding our hearts through the Spirit which God has given us (cf. Rom. 5:5). On the basis of their authentic subjectivity, applied to the Christian tradition, Christians find out what they are to believe; *foundations,* applied to the fruit of *dialectic,* yields *doctrines.* Thus by attending to their tradition Christians come to know "of the Spirit that is given to us, of the Son who redeemed us, of the Father who sent the Son and with the Son sends the Spirit, and of our future destiny when we shall know, not as in a glass darkly, but face to face" (cf. 1 Cor. 13). They also come to know their task within the world. "As human authenticity promotes progress, and human unauthenticity generates decline, so Christian authenticity—which is a love of others that does not shrink from self-sacrifice and suffering—is the sovereign means for . . . overcoming evil with good" (Rom. 12:21)—something which constantly needs doing, it should be added, in the Church as well as in the world (Lonergan 1972, 291).

Of course, it is up to the Christian theologian, not to the methodologist as such, to show that in speaking of one's religious experience in terms of God, or of Christ, one is liable to be speaking the truth. It is one thing to *describe* the nature of the task which is *foundations;* it is another to *perform* it; and it is vital, if everything is to be intellectually and morally above board, that the two activities should not be confused with one another. To *describe foundations* is not to beg the question, against Theravada Buddhism or secular humanism, of the existence of God, or against Judaism and Islam, of the divinity of Christ.[14] To *do foundations,* as a Christian theologian, would be to show the nature of the fully active intellect and completely clear conscience which will accept the basic Christian *doctrines,* having fairly evaluated the salient alternatives through the process of *dialectic.*

[14] For misunderstanding on this point, see pp. 42–43 below.

# Chapter 3

# OBJECTIONS TO THE METHOD

A number of objections to Lonergan's method have been published. In what follows, I shall list the most significant of them, and evaluate them one by one.

(i) *Lonergan's methodological principles are too restrictive.* Brian Hebblethwaite has written: "Within the overall intention to think through the world-view that has come down to us in each religious tradition, any and every critical method must be tried out and pursued as far as it will go. We cannot prescribe a single pattern" (Hebblethwaite 1980, 19). But I think this is to underestimate the generality of Lonergan's proposals. Does this critic really propose that we should be prepared to do other than attend to the relevant data, think up hypotheses to account for them, reasonably judge which of these hypotheses is most likely to be true, and responsibly decide to act accordingly, in our theological proceedings? Such a proposal could hardly be taken seriously. But if the critic is demanding that theologians should aspire to be *unrestrictedly* attentive, intelligent, reasonable, and responsible, then this is precisely what Lonergan's method requires of them. If he is maintaining that Lonergan's proposals fail to meet these very general requirements, or that the requirements do not issue in the functional specialties in the manner that Lonergan argues, then it does not seem to me that he has supported this claim.

In fact, it is the very comprehensiveness of Lonergan's method which seems to have provided ground for the complaint of "the confusing alternation in his work between empiricist and classical rationalist approaches and solutions" (Shea 1976, 410).[1] This complaint seems simply to bypass the main argument of *Insight*, which is that empiricism and rationalism provide opposite and one-sided accounts of the nature of knowledge and reality, both of which have to be taken account of in a satisfactory epistemology or metaphysics.

(ii) *The appeal to introspection, which is central to Lonergan's method, has been shown by contemporary analytical philosophers to be mistaken in principle.* There is no doubt that many contemporary analytical philosophers are hostile to introspection. I think Lonergan would attribute this to their

---

[1] This is not the only instance among these objections where one is forcefully reminded of Mark 14:56 and parallels.

assimilation of all senses of "introspection" to the sense in which he himself admits that it is "just myth" (Lonergan 1972, 8). It is undeniable that, on Lonergan's account, the exploration and full exploitation of our capacity to know does involve something that would usually be termed "introspection." It is probably for this reason in particular that Patrick McGrath dismisses his whole program as "language gone on holiday" (Corcoran 1975, 34). It is worth noting that every significant advance in science or philosophy, and every original achievement in literature, involves the use of terms in new collocations for new purposes, and can thus be dismissed, by those so disposed, as "language gone on holiday."

On the more substantive issue, one is inclined to raise the following question. Has this critic ever been aware of being puzzled by an experience, of hitting on some possible explanation of it, of judging that there is sufficient reason to believe that the explanation is probably correct, or probably incorrect? If he is ever aware of carrying out these kinds of activity, and will advert to what he is thus aware of (thus engaging in "introspection" in the sense demanded by Lonergan), he will have some idea of what Lonergan, whether right or wrong, is talking about. I fail to understand what it would be to carry out these kinds of activity without being aware of them. If he never carries them out at all, it is difficult to see why he should be taken seriously on this topic, or indeed on any other. What is the point of talking to someone who has never come to understand anything about which he was previously puzzled and has consequently never enjoyed an "act of understanding" in Lonergan's sense?[2] I cannot judge whether Lonergan may be said to have "examined the concept of knowing" (Corcoran 1975, 34), but he has arguably made the most detailed and searching examination by any contemporary philosopher of what it is to know and to come to know, and it may not implausibly be claimed that this is a more profitable enterprise. You do not get far in ornithology by examining the concept of a greenfinch.

I do think that a sound if superficial objection may be made against Lonergan, that knowing as such is hardly an activity. It was true an hour ago that I knew that there was no such person as Father Christmas, though I was not exerting my mind about the matter at all. Often those trained in analytical philosophy would learn more from Lonergan if, when he writes about "knowing," they would take him to be referring to "coming to know."

When the dust of merely verbal controversy has settled, I think that the central issue between Lonergan and many analytical philosophers on the philosophy of mind may be seen to be as follows. Wittgenstein and his followers rightly emphasise that language is primarily a public and interpersonal affair. They argue cogently that there would be no place in human language for such "private" entities as thoughts and feelings, unless the occurrence of these were characteristically accompanied by "public" events

---

[2] Cf. Lonergan's demonstration of the self-destructiveness of behaviorism, quoted above.

such as noises and gestures (Wittgenstein 1953, 1, 243–45). But this doctrine as it stands is not in the least incompatible with Lonergan's philosophy of mind. Indeed, Lonergan makes much the same point in his own way when he says that the real, public and interpersonal world is what judgments are primarily about.[3] Wittgenstein is surely right about what is necessary if we are to acquire a preliminary conception of the meaning of such terms as "wonder," "inquire," "understand," and so on. But why should not introspection, at least in one sense of the term, be useful if we are to gain a more adequate conception of wonder, inquiry, and understanding themselves?

To take an analogy, the ordinary person's concept of "silver" is one thing, that of the trained chemist another. In one sense, ordinary persons know exactly what silver is. In another sense, they do not know it at all, and cannot come to know it without learning some chemistry. The chemist's conception of silver is not, of course, totally unrelated to that of the ordinary person. It is derived from it by a series of questions, hypotheses, observations, and experiments. On Lonergan's view, much the same applies if one wishes to progress from the elementary conceptions of wondering, understanding and so on, implicit in ordinary language, to which what Wittgenstein says certainly applies, to a more systematic and critical account. Inquiry, hypothesis, and observation are to be applied to the data provided by one's own conscious activities. Do I ever come to understand as a result of inquiry? Apparently, however stupid I am, I just occasionally do. Do I ever wonder whether my understanding is correct, and judge on sufficient reason that it is or is not? Inasmuch as I do, I not only possess a degree of intelligence, but a smattering of reasonableness as well. Do I ever decide to act in accordance with what is true and good, rather than following immediate impulses of desire or fear, or capitulating to anxiety or ambition? If so, I am to that extent responsible in addition. If Lonergan is right, we not only *can* attend to our intellectual, rational, and moral consciousness, but we *ought* to do so if we are to cope with a number of long-standing problems in philosophy. It is not obvious that the arguments of Wittgenstein and his followers have proved that either proposition is untenable.

(iii) *Lonergan's treatment of the problem of objectivity in science and in human inquiry in general is inadequate* (Corcoran 1975, 68–71). One of Lonergan's disciples might well suggest, on the contrary, that one of his greatest achievements as a philosopher is to solve that problem of objectivity which has been so constantly a stumbling-block to philosophers since Descartes.[4] One could hardly expect those who have managed to satisfy themselves with some form of naive realism at one extreme, or with subjectivism

---

[3] For a brief treatment of this criticism by Lonergan himself, see Lonergan 1972, 254–57.

[4] The solution to the problem of objectivity may be said to have been adumbrated by Peirce, Collingwood, and Popper, but nowhere so clearly and distinctly set out as by Lonergan in *Insight*. Cf. Collingwood 1939, 33, 37; Peirce 1958, 27–29, 35, 39–40, 51; Popper 1972, chap. I; Lonergan 1957, chap. 13.

or relativism at the other, to be content with Lonergan's solution. According to Lonergan, the cardinal error on this topic is the assumption that objectivity is always somehow a matter of taking a look at what is there rather than, as he himself argues, of asking and answering all relevant questions about the data available to sensation or consciousness. Since neither causality, nor other minds, nor the things and events of the past are capable of being looked at, a consistent application of this principle, far from vindicating the naive realism which is its starting-point, would turn virtually the whole world which had previously seemed to be real into a mental construction (Russell 1956, 269–80). The solution to the problem is this. Although we cannot take a look at the past, other minds, the theoretical entities postulated by scientists, and so on, at least our judgments about them, come to as a result of asking questions, can be *verified* in experience.[5]

For example, there is no way in which I can conceivably take a look at King Darius' intentions on the eve of the Battle of Gaugamela, but I may find one possibility about the matter more confirmed than others by contemporary reports, whose meaning in turn I must reach by a process of hypothesis and deduction from a sensory "given" of marks on paper, scratches on stones and scraps of metal, noises emitted by professors of ancient history, and so on. According to Lonergan, this capacity to ask questions about a set of data, and to frame hypotheses and form judgments accordingly, is what is relevant above all if one is to grasp the nature of objectivity. To be "objective" is nothing other than to give full rein to one's "subjective" capacity to attend to evidence, and to go on asking questions until it is fully explained. Mary Hesse has no patience with the view that the ultimate court of justification is nothing other than a full deployment of each person's innate capacity to look for and to find sufficient reason (Corcoran 1976, 68–71).[6] But where would *she* place the final court of appeal? In confrontation with the Brute Facts Out There? Or in submission to arbitrarily selected or imposed authority? How else could one non-arbitarily determine the facts, or select the relevant authority, except by use to the full of a native capacity which is at least in general outline such as Lonergan describes?

According to Professor Torrance, in his fine discussion of Lonergan's method, since "the immense revolution in the foundations of thought that

---

[5] Cf. the "canons of empirical method" distinguished by Lonergan (1957, chap. 3), which have their analogue in interpretation (586–91). The "canon of selection," which lays it down that only explanations which can be confirmed by sensation belong to empirical science, easily twists into the error that only the objects of sensation really exist.

[6] Incidentally, it should be clear to the unprejudiced reader that Lonergan is not "knocking logic" in the passage cited to that effect by Mary Hesse (Lonergan 1972, 77; Lonergan 1975, 72). Cf. Lonergan 1972, 6, 66, 85, 94, 305; Lonergan 1957, 276–277, 508, 576–77. As is clear from many passages in his work, Lonergan is merely insisting that logic should be envisaged in the wider context of what he calls "method." That logic in the strict sense is a *necessary*, but not *sufficient* means, for arriving at the truth about things, would be universally agreed among philosophers.

has come to light with relativity theory we allow the field we are investigating to disclose itself to us in accordance with its own nature and in the light of its own internal relations" (Corcoran 1975, 123).[7] He proposes that we should apply the moral to theology. But is it really the case the contemporary physics presupposes some kind of direct intuition of the fundamental nature of things? Or have its theories been arrived at as a result of a series of questions put to an increasingly wide range of data, with theories accepted provisionally, rejected, or modified accordingly? The former view, which appears to be Professor Torrance's, seems to be false as a matter of historical as well as epistemological fact. Lonergan holds the latter view and plausibly suggests that, in its general outlines at least, it is as applicable to theology as to natural science.

(iv) *The result of Lonergan's preoccupation with epistemology is an unsatisfactory metaphysics* (Shea 1976, 274). The case against all those thinkers who, following the lead of J. Maréchal, have tried to found a traditional type of metaphysics on a transcendental basis, has been argued in an article by J. B. Reichmann (Reichman 1968). Those who wish to provide such a basis, says Reichmann, point out that metaphysics starts with a question about the nature of reality. However, he answers, the same is true of all sciences, and indeed of all branches of knowledge; it is in no way peculiar to metaphysics. Thus to relate metaphysics to questioning fails to indicate what the metaphysician does "that no one else does, and no one else can do" (Reichmann 1968, 456–57).

It is true that all the sciences, natural and human, are a matter of putting questions to a range of data. But this does not imply that the metaphysician may not be concerned with questioning in a particular way. According to Lonergan, and to the other thinkers who are in basic agreement with him on this matter, what the metaphysician asks questions about is the fact that the world can come to be known by questioning; the metaphysician tries to determine what is to be inferred from this about its overall nature and structure. On this view, reality, or the concrete universe, is what is *to be known* by the process of questioning; it exists prior to the questioning and the justified true judgments in which this culminates. It is thus unfair to maintain, as Reichmann does (following G. Siewerth), that the "transcendental method transforms the knowing subject into the ground of reality, and

---

[7] Cf. J. P. Mackey's remark that to be a scientist is a matter of allowing one's method to be dictated by one's subject matter (Corcoran 1975, 162). Lonergan would concede that this was true in a sense—it follows from his principles, in fact—but would insist all the same that there were methodological principles which apply to all fields. There are few sciences where one makes progress by brushing aside relevant evidence, or by failing to envisage or test hypotheses. It is interesting to compare aspersions on Lonergan's method derived from the sophisticated naive realism—if one may use such an expression—of Torrance and Mackey, with those based on the tendencies to extreme and self-destructive relativism in Hesse and Lash. Cf. note 1 above.

reality itself into the product of the judgmental affirmation" (Reichmann 1968, 461). The subject comes to know something of the world, and adverts to the fact that a certain structure of cognitive acts is involved in doing so; from this structure the subject makes inferences about the reality which existed *before* these cognitive acts and *independently of* them, but whose overall nature is all the same to be determined by the fact that it is nothing other than what either *is* known or *is to be known* by means of them. So much for the objection to the transcendental grounding of metaphysics. And metaphysics does need such grounding. Short of it, it inevitably gets "bogged down in a pre-critical morass" (Lonergan 1974, 25). The supposition of any real thing or state of affairs which is not in some actual or possible relation to inquiry, and to the understanding and judgment in which this issues, is incoherent. So much at least should surely be conceded to the sceptical and empiricist strands in modern philosophy which are often regarded as destructive of traditional metaphysics.[8]

In this connection, the suggestion has been made that Lonergan's notions of and attitude to science are somewhat old-fashioned (Corcoran 1975, 59). It is true that Lonergan shares with Sir Karl Popper, and I would have thought with the majority of scientists, the opinion that scientists are engaged in trying to find out what is really so. He would also agree with Popper that scientific doctrines cannot be certain; that they approach towards the truth so far as they survive stringent testing in relation to the evidence which might falsify them.[9] If to be up with the times on these matters is to have espoused the relativism associated with the name of Thomas Kuhn, then it is worth pointing out that Lonergan has re-iterated, in terms of his own philosophical principles, the traditional arguments to the effect that such a relativism is self-destructive.[10] Kuhn has in fact repudiated as a travesty of his own position that relativism associated with him, protesting that his view entails only that logic and experience alone are in some cases insufficient to adjudicate between rival scientific theories.[11] With this Lonergan would be in

[8] On Lonergan's account of metaphysics and its basis in cognitional theory, see Lonergan 1957, chaps. 11–17.

[9] The comparison of Lonergan and Popper on science, metaphysics and the theory of knowledge is highly instructive. Cf. Popper, 13–18, 50–51, chap. 3; 83–83, 300–4, chap. 13.

[10] Mary Hesse writes that "recent developments in the philosophy of science strongly suggest that" the claim, supported by Lonergan, that science approaches closer and closer to the truth about the matters with which it deals, "was only an unstable resting-point between classical nineteenth-century confidence and late twentieth-century scepticism and relativism" (Corcoran 1975, 62). One is inclined to retort that, however lunatic the fashions which may afflict the philosophy of science in the latter half of the twentieth century, the classical arguments against scepticism and relativism will go on recommending themselves to anyone who is interested in finding out what is true.

[11] The basic trouble with the kind of relativism attributable to Kuhn is briefly this. It applies to natural science, but is based on historical arguments. If the historical arguments are sound, they presuppose a non-sceptical and non-relativist attitude in historical studies—that is to say,

complete agreement, since he emphasises the indispensable role of understanding and judgment in coming to know what is the case, whether in
science or elsewhere.

(v) *Although Lonergan has been at pains to stress the diversity of human
cultures, he still underestimates the discontinuity between them* (Corcoran
1975, 127). In making this criticism, Nicholas Lash does admit that a certain
identity in basic human mental capacities and dispositions must be assumed
(Corcoran 1975, 135), and I believe that when Lonergan tries to set out a
transcendental base for theology, he has done nothing other than spell out
these basic human capacities clearly and distinctly. It is indeed difficult to
see how, short of some experience, understanding, judgment, and decision,
a being could be human in anything like the normal sense, let alone be
capable of constructing monuments and leaving records able to be interpreted by historians or archaeologists. On the basis of these alleged features
common to all human mental life, Lonergan has attempted to show how what
was originally expressed in terms of one culture can be re-expressed in terms
intelligible to another. One wonders whether this critic would wish to claim
that cultures are so discontinuous that no identity of meaning can ever be
established between what is said within the context of one and what is said
within the context of another. If this were true, Christianity as such would be
based on a mistake, inasmuch as it involves the communication of a message
originally received in one particular culture to human beings of all cultures
whatever (Matt. 28:19); and the same will apply *a fortiori* to that reflection of
Christian faith which is Christian theology. In any case, the thesis has
awkward consequences apart from the falsity of Christianity. It invalidates all
anthropology, and all history which is concerned with cultures other than
that from which the historian comes, for these disciplines are aimed at
discovering what human beings of other cultures meant by their words and
actions, by the documents they composed and the monuments they left.

I infer, then, that this critic's thesis is hardly so extreme as to imply that
we cannot hope to apprehend what is meant by persons of cultures widely
different from our own. But in that case, *how* do we or can we set about doing
so? Can we set out the basic mental operations involved? It appears to me
that once one has fairly grasped the problem, one is more or less constrained

---

that we can really find out by investigation what persons in times and places other than our own
did, said, and meant. But if this is so, one of two possibilities seems to follow. Either, as Popper
has in effect suggested, the science of history must be more objective than that of, say, physics
(Lakatos and Musgrave, 1970, 57–58); or Kuhn has refuted the basis for his own position rather
than that which he is trying to attack. On Lonergan's account, the method which Kuhn rightly,
and more or less inevitably, presupposes in his historical inquiries will apply, with appropriate
modifications, to physics and chemistry as well. Cf. Lonergan 1972, 4. For Kuhn's repudiation of
the relativism often attributed to him, or at any rate inferred from what he says, see Lakatos and
Musgrave 1970, 234.

to give an answer at least approximately the same as Lonergan's. Do we not have to be *attentive* to the writings and monuments left by the cultures concerned, and to the gestures and noises made by their members insofar as these are available to us here and now? Must we not also exercise our *intelligence* in thinking of the range of things that they might have meant by what they were doing? Should we not then be as *reasonable* as possible in provisionally preferring among this range of things the one that best accords with the evidence available to our senses? And do we not hope to discover, as a result of the whole operation, how the persons concerned spoke and acted with more or less intelligence, reason, and so on?

(vi) *In spite of Lonergan's explicit repudiation of "classicism," much of his work shows that he has not outgrown it* (Shea 1976, 275). So far as I can see, those who have made this objection have failed to distinguish properly between what Lonergan calls "classicism" and the use of technical terminology necessary for what he calls *systematics*. *Systematics* is basically a matter of carrying out Anselm's program of "faith seeking understanding". The systematician is trying to determine how the doctrines of faith cohere with one another, and how they are significant for the whole business of human living. It is of the very nature of such understanding, as is illustrated by the example of natural science quite as much as by that of Scholastic theology, that once it has passed a certain stage of development it needs a technical language in which it may be expressed. One of the main uses of *systematics* is to demonstrate how one religious faith may be expressed in a wide range of ways according to the different cultures of those who believe and live by it. It provides a viewpoint which is potentially transcultural, much as Euclidean geometry or modern chemistry is so. Anyone with sufficient education in any culture can grasp the theorems and deductions involved. It is convenient to use the original technical terms to express these theorems and deductions, and it is presumably the resulting persistence of this terminology over time which has given rise to the misapprehension that *systematics* is essentially bound up with "classicism." While "classicism" is the belief or assumption that there is but one culture, and is very apt to issue in insistence on uniformity of expression, a non-classicist *systematics* can discern and therefore accept a unity of belief within a wide variety of forms of expression.

Although Lonergan deplores "classicism," he emphasises the importance of *systematics*. Chapter 19 of *Insight*, which is alleged to be especially symptomatic of the "classicism" which Lonergan has not outgrown, develops an argument for the existence of God. Such arguments, if they are to be rigorous rather than merely rhetorical and shoddy, necessarily involve the kind of exact and unequivocal definition of terms which is the special prerogative of *systematics*. Nowhere does the chapter display the properly "classicist" presupposition that there is only one culture, or imply that its arguments can be presented and grasped only by those who share that culture.[12] Someone might ask why theologians should be bothered with *systematics*, once they have dispensed with the "classicism" with which it is admittedly often associated. Reasons why they should have already been mentioned,[13] and it may be added that if theologians are to be fully reasonable and responsible, they ought to be concerned with the question of whether there is good reason to believe in God, and in the basic tenets of their religion, rather than evading the issue by talking of leaps of faith or by claiming that religion is a game played with rules quite peculiar to itself. But insofar as they are concerned to produce sound arguments, as opposed to mere rhetorical suasions, in favor of their beliefs, they will be concerned to be precise in the definition of their terms, and to set out clearly the process by which the conclusions may be inferred from the premises. Such concerns are of the essence of *systematics*.

Thus *systematics* is not dependent on "classicism," and it is important to pursue the former without being committed to the latter.

(vii) *The method is not sufficiently specific to theology* (Shea 1976, 274). Notable among those who have made this objection is Karl Rahner (Rahner 1971). It is true that Lonergan in effect describes a general method for getting to know what is true and what is good, and tries to show that this method has a special application to theology in the sense of reflection on religion.[14] In short he is applying a method of general application to the particular instance of theology. I would argue that such a procedure is not only *harmless* but *strictly necessary* if one is to have a fully critical theology, capable in principle of answering any question relevant to the topic which may arise. Among the questions relevant to religion is whether all religious beliefs are illusory, and among those relevant to theism whether there exists any God at all. A method in theology which is so specialised that it does not allow such questions to be asked, and to be answered in terms of an intelligence and reasonableness which do not somehow beg these questions, is less than comprehensively critical. If it is urged that such questions cannot be asked from a point of view of neutrality, since religion, or Christianity, has a rationality which is entirely *sui generis*, it is difficult to see why the same might not be urged on behalf of any kind of belief whatever, however absurd. Once one concedes that even the most basic presuppositions of religion have to be argued for, it is hard to see how one could deny that this can only be

[12] In his later writings, Lonergan has expressed some misgivings about this chapter (e.g., Lonergan 1974, 277).

[13] See pp. 24–25 above.

[14] The first chapter of *Method* outlines the means of finding out what is so. The topics discussed in these chapters do thus seem to provide the "background" necessary for a method in theology—given that the object of such a method is to find out what other people have said and meant on the topic of religion, and how much of this actually is so. As to the second chapter—people may properly wonder what good religion is, if any, and how it is related for better or worse to other goods of human life. It is thus suitable that the "background" to the method should include a chapter entitled "The Human Good."

done by appeal to general principles of rational belief and responsible assent which are applicable to all doctrines and opinions, whether religious or otherwise. That these general principles have to be applied to particular phenomena, and that these applications have to yield particular results, for there to be "theology" properly speaking, is never denied by Lonergan either explicitly or by implication.

(viii) *Lonergan's principle, that all those who engage in the second phase of theology be subject to religious conversion, renders it impossible usefully to discuss religious doctrines across the frontiers between different religions, or across the frontier between religion and irreligion. But such discussion is an essential part of theology* (Hebblethwaite 1980, 18–19; Corcoran 1975, 98). It ought to be insisted that "theology be discussed without reservations in the context of critical rationality" (Corcoran 1975, 98). This I believe to be one of the most telling objections to the method, and I shall accordingly devote a fair amount of space to its discussion. Briefly, Lonergan would completely agree with Hebblethwaite and Pannenberg that every theological statement should be subjected to the most rigorous and extensive possible rational criticism, and that the arguments of atheists and of those of other religions should be most scrupulously taken into account. However, his remarks about religious conversion as a prerequisite for the second phase of theology do seem to conflict with this (Lonergan 1972, 268).

One misunderstanding which seems to underlie the criticism is relatively easy to clear up. The essence of "religious conversion," as set forth in Lonergan's later writings, is a being in love which *naturally issues in* acceptance of *some* set of religious doctrines, but does not *strictly entail* this. Clearly, then, if one keeps strictly to what Lonergan writes in *Method in Theology*, persons might be religiously converted while being and remaining Muslims or Buddhists; and one might possibly even be religiously converted while being and remaining a secularist atheist (Lonergan 1972, 278). "Religious conversion" as Lonergan conceives it appears to me to amount in practice to a sort of basic good will—an absence at a deep level of "the great refusal" which cannot be bothered with accepting fundamental responsibility for one's life, because it is less trouble to flow along with the stream of one's own pleasures and dislikes and of the prejudices of one's group.[15] At any rate, it is certainly wrong to infer from the proposition that only the religiously converted can engage in the second phase of theology the proposition that only Christians are to be listened to in the second phase of Christian theology.

And yet, even when this misunderstanding has been cleared away, the objection does retain some force, if only with respect to terminology. An

[15] What amounts to "religious conversion" in this sense, and the way in which it may fail to issue in explicit religious belief, has been excellently described by Karl Rahner (Rahner 1978, 60–61, 98).

example may serve to sharpen the issue. What would one say of Andrei Sakharov—assuming (what is perhaps denied in some circles) that he is a man passionately devoted to goodness and truth, even at the cost of great hardship to himself, and assuming that he is without positive religious beliefs in the usual sense? Is he "religiously converted," or is he not? That he is grasped thoroughly and splendidly by whatever it is that promotes intellectual and moral authenticity seems to me too obvious to merit discussion. But he is not "religiously converted" in the usual sense of the expression, and it seems to me very misleading to adapt the usual terminology in such a way as to make it appear that he is.

Several elements, which are at least conceptually separable from one another, seem to be involved in "religious conversion" in Lonergan's sense: (i) a change of horizon which leads naturally and in normal cases to acceptance of specifically religious doctrines; (ii) the basic good will which supplies the foundation of a life committed to coming to know what is true, and coming to know and do what is good; (iii) God's gift of love. In speaking as he does of "religious conversion," Lonergan in effect assumes that these three are actually identical.[16] This is perhaps justifiable in the work of a methodologist making proposals which are in the first instance directed to theologians who believe in God, and are therefore likely to share this assumption. But *very many* in our culture maintain that a sincere and rigorous application of a person's intellectual powers abetted by a moral sense will lead to a rejection of all positive religious beliefs, including belief that there is a God, and as a result would hold that (ii) is far from identical with (i), and consequently cannot be interpreted as (iii). If Lonergan's method is in principle, as I believe it is and can be shown to be, one by which all religious and irreligious positions may fairly be compared with one another and assessed, it will not do to seem to prejudge with issue by the very terminology that one uses. The paradox here, of course, is that Lonergan has provided impressive arguments on those very topics which he may seem to foreclose, and has in fact been interpreted as foreclosing. He has argued that a comprehensive rationality is likely to confirm belief in God and in Christ, and submission to the Catholic Church.

Even talk of "conversion" in unequivocally approving terms may be felt by many to beg the question of the truth of religion or of some religion. Accordingly, I would make the tentative proposal that when the method is used in a fully ecumenical context, Lonergan's own way of talking about "conversion" should be dropped. Instead of referring to "moral conversion," the theologian should point out how it is universally presupposed—and quite correctly, often in defiance of philosophical positions tenaciously main-

---

[16] What is involved in this assumption is beautifully expressed by Donald Evans: "I link together religion and morality through their common origin: divine activity in authentically human individuals who are receptive" (Evans 1980, 7).

tained—that one is the better for turning away from exclusive concern with satisfaction to the realisation of objective values, which include the satisfaction of others. Instead of speaking of "intellectual conversion," which may be felt to beg the question in favor of Lonergan's own philosophical principles, and which in any case would be rejected out of hand by most contemporary philosophers, I propose that one should make detailed appeal to the self-destructive consequence of philosophical positions other than critical realism, and to the working-out of the principles of critical realism in ethics, metaphysics, hermeneutics, and theology. (This, of course, is precisely what is done so thoroughly in *Insight*.) Instead of "religious conversion," I suggest that reference be made, where a compendious phrase is needed, to something like "basic good will" or "basic authenticity."

As Lonergan says, a contemporary Catholic theology must address itself not only to Christians, but to non-Christians and atheists (Lonergan 1974, 62). My terminological worries are related precisely to this point. No intellectual and moral type is more typical of our time than the well-educated person who sincerely believes that thoroughly to follow through one's intellectual powers and one's moral sense is to be led to repudiate religious belief. "What is religion," asks Lonergan rhetorically, "but complete self-transcendence?" (Lonergan 1974, 129). Well, as a matter of fact, what goes by the name of religion is many other things besides the intellectual and moral authenticity which are self-transcendence in Lonergan's sense, very often does not include them, and not infrequently is actually inimical to them. To embrace or to continue in a religion is at least sometimes to repudiate the promptings of one's intellect and to cling to individual and group bias in morals and in politics. Those who believe religion to be at best irrelevant, at worse inimical, to cognitional and moral self-transcendence, have to be convinced of the contrary, even if their intellectual thoroughness and moral integrity, as any Christian theologian would hold, are in the last analysis to be identified as themselves the fruit of God's gift of love.

Why, it may be asked, does Lonergan use the terminology that he does, if the nature of the method is really as I have described it? One reason seems to be that it is at least rather unusual for people to be convinced by rigorous arguments that they ought to become the adherent of one of the religions, before they do so. It is far more usual, for example, for those who have already embraced a theistic religion to construct and accept arguments for the existence of God. The kind of process which one might infer from *Insight* to be the norm, whereby a person attends to the nature of knowledge, works out the appropriate metaphysical and ethical position, and then goes on—as it were entirely out of the blue—to ask whether there is good reason to believe that there is a God, is presumably somewhat rare.

Further, Lonergan has argued, in writings subsequent to *Insight*, that "natural theology" and *systematics*, the working-out of arguments for the existence of God on the basis of his "generalised empirical method" on the one hand, and a systematic exposition and explanation of what is affirmed by one's religious tradition on the other, ought to be engaged in together rather than separately. If this maxim is adhered to, it will be clearer than it has often been in the past that the God with whom one has to do in one's religion is the same being as the God for whose existence philosophical arguments may be proposed, and there will be less pretext for Pascal's misleading antithesis between "the God of Abraham, Isaac and Jacob" and "the god of the philosophers." And theology and philosophy will be able to combine forces to mutual advantage, the former ensuring that religious content, the latter that systematic rigor, are never lost sight of.[17] Lonergan has actually stated that his own arguments for God's existence, in chapter 19 of *Insight,* gives a somewhat misleading view because they are not set in the context of a systematic theology.[18] But if the considerations which I have adduced in the last few paragraphs are not entirely off the mark, a case can to be made for regressing somewhat towards the point of view of *Insight* from that of *Method,* at least when the theologian is trying to communicate with the secularist of good will. The task of convincing such persons that there are after all good reasons for believing in God under some description, and that of expounding systematically who and what the God is who is known and loved in the religious tradition, are worth distinguishing. Those who were really expert in the former field, though they would be much the worse off for lacking a working knowledge of the other, could hardly be as expert in that. To a degree, I am saying, in contradiction to Lonergan, there must not only be "distinction" between the two tasks, but "separation" as well, even though Lonergan is surely right that the separation has gone much too far in the Catholic theology of the last few centuries, where *De Deo Uno* has been treated as a strictly philosophical topic, *De Deo Trino* as a strictly theological one.[19]

(ix) *It is unclear how the question of God, and its answer, are related to the functional specialties* (Shea 1976, 281). Lonergan situates the question of God and its answer in relation to *all* the functional specialties. Our predecessors have spoken and written about God, and we want to make up our minds about God. We do *research* to find out exactly what our predecessors spoke

[17] On this matter, see Lonergan 1973 a, *passim;* 1972, 335–40.

[18] See "*Insight* Revisited" (Lonergan 1974, 263–78).

[19] The authority of Thomas Aquinas is often invoked for the separation, but, as Lonergan says, his own recommendation of distinction without separation in fact conforms to Aquinas' practice. This may be seen from the manner in which treatment of the one God and of the Trinity are woven together in the *Prima Pars* of the *Summa Theologica,* and the way in which the latter is introduced. Aquinas freely makes use of the sources of revelation in the former, and of his philosophical principles in the latter, even though he maintains that the central theses of the former can be established without appeal to the data of revelation, in a manner that those of the latter cannot. In insisting that the one God should not be discussed by Christian theologians in isolation from the triune God of revelation, Lonergan is following a well-established fashion among contemporary theologians. See O'Donnell 1982, 166.

and wrote on the subject; *interpretation* to determine what each of them meant in doing so; *history* to connect their words, writings, and meanings about God into a connected narrative of their attitudes to and beliefs about God; *dialectic* to establish to what extent these attitudes and beliefs were well or ill-founded, properly or improperly motivated. In *foundations* we try to articulate what it is to be conscious subjects asking questions about God. In *doctrines* we apply this to the results of the previous functional specialties so that we may determine what we are to believe about God. In *systematics* we seek to gain a comprehensive understanding of our beliefs about God, of their coherence, and of their relevance to the rest of human living and believing. In *communications* we strive to express the beliefs about God so understood to persons of every sort and condition in terms which will make sense to them.

(x)  *In "Method in Theology", Lonergan presupposes the truth of Catholic doctrines, including that of the existence of God. But the truth of Catholic doctrine has to be demonstrated.* David Tracy expresses his view of "the foundational task" of theology in a series of questions: "How does one uncover the referent of the dimension of ultimacy in human experience? Is the Christian and theistic explication of this dimension the right one? How does one validate the religious and Christian claims to represent the dimension of ultimacy in the face of a Marxist or Naturalist thematization?" He then adds that these are precisely the questions not faced by Lonergan (Shea 1976, 279).

These questions would be answered by a clear articulation of what is meant by "God," by an argument to the effect that there is a God, and by another argument for the truth of specifically Christian claims. So far from its being the case that none of these questions is faced by Lonergan, answers to all of them are presented and argued for, notably in chapters 19 and 20 of *Insight*. The whole epistemological and metaphysical argument of the book, which culminates in these chapters, is such as to demonstrate that "Marxist and naturalist thematizations," which either fail to raise the question of God at all or give a negative answer to the question, are inadequate. But procedures of this kind are not merely a matter of "foundations" in Lonergan's sense. They are also concerned with *doctrines*—for example that God exists—and *systematics*—which involves the kind of precise definition of terms which makes serious and soundly-based argument for God's existence possible. Although Tracy is surely right about the importance of what he calls "the foundational task," he is quite wrong to say that Lonergan has not faced it.

Another critic makes the charge that Lonergan's procedure is circular, that he justifies his results by his method, and his method by his results.[20] Lonergan does, in fact, base his method on his cognitional theory, and he

---

[20] E. McLaren writes that "the circularity is staggering" (Corcoran 1975, 80). An unkind counter-critic might make a similar assessment of the misinterpretation.

proposes that the cognitional theory in turn should be tested by each reader's attention to the data provided by empirical, intellectual, rational, and moral consciousness. Theologians are to obtain their results by applying the method thus acquired to the data provided by the religious traditions within which they work. What I think has misled both critics is this. Lonergan does not purport to *perform* "the foundational task" in *Method in Theology*. The principal aim of the book is to *describe* a method of doing theology, and to advance reasons for holding that the method is the right one. To argue for the truth of theistic or Christian or Catholic doctrine would be to *apply* the method. If one wants to know what, in Lonergan's opinion, is to be gained by *applying* the method, one should read the last two chapters and the epilogue of *Insight*, as well as the Latin treatises *De Deo Trino* and *De Verbo Incarnato*. The last three chapters of *Method in Theology*, those on *doctrines*, *systematics* and *communications*, take Catholic doctrines as examples of statements on religious matters which someone may wish to affirm, understand, and communicate to others. The same could have been done with the doctrines of any other religion (or, *mutatis mutandis*, any anti-religious system of ideas), denomination, or sect. Tracy claims that Lonergan's discovery in the Christian tradition of an adequate thematization of religious conversion is "dogmatic and not critical" (Shea 1976, 278). But this is to neglect the facts that it was not the task of *Method in Theology* to justify Christian doctrines, and that Lonergan has done this exhaustively elsewhere. The point of the book was not to argue for Lonergan's own religious beliefs, but to argue for a method of arguing for any set of religious or irreligious beliefs.

It should be clear that the answer to this objection has an important bearing on that to the seventh. To raise fundamental questions of the kind Tracy alludes to one needs a method which goes against Rahner's requirement precisely by *not* being merely specific to theology.

(xi) *The method is of little use because its effect is to put everyone in the right* (Corcoran 1975, 81). It is of some interest that another critic reproaches Lonergan for maintaining that even such theological giants as Barth and Bultmann have not "arrived" (Corcoran 1975, 72). No doubt controversialists will see this disposition of Lonergan, at once to give prizes to everyone and to disqualify nearly everyone, as proof of his inconsistency. Others may perhaps venture to wonder whether the explanation is not that the interpretation of at least one of these critics is flawed. This hypothesis is confirmed by a reading of *Method in Theology*, especially in conjunction with *Insight* and Lonergan's Latin theological treatises. The effect of Lonergan's principles is to *invite* all interested parties to participate in the theological activity of *dialectic*. One may contrast Karl Barth, whose theological principles exclude *a limine* effective contribution to the subject by atheists, or indeed by those theists who deny that, or even question whether, God is uniquely revealed in Christ (Barth 1936–64, 1, 2, 172; 2, 1, 86; 1959, 69). Barth rules out argument against atheists on their own ground, which attempts to show that it is intelligent and reasonable for them to come to believe in God, as "natural theology," and an affront to God's gracious self-revelation. That these doctrines, along with all other beliefs whether religious or otherwise, ought to be questioned, ought to command one's assent only so far as one has sufficient reason to bestow it, is a consequence of what Lonergan calls "intellectual conversion." Thus his statement that Barth and Bultmann are not "intellectually converted" has a determinate meaning, whether it is true or false, and is not a mere gesture of dismissal (Corcoran 1976, 72. Cf. Lonergan 1972, 318, 238–40).

To be invited to the field of dialectic, along with all interested parties, is one thing; genuinely to accept the invitation is another thing; to leave the field unscathed another still. In fact, as anyone who dips into *Insight* or *De Deo Trino* finds out pretty quickly, the dialectical field is littered with corpses. Lonergan deliberately refrains from *using* the weapons in *Method in Theology*. I think this is why some have reproached the work for lacking any serious philosophical argument; he merely shows his principles to theologians, and gives them some instruction in their use. A hall of instruction in the use of weaponry is not the same as the field of battle. It is most unlikely that the position of any theologian will be unaffected by their use; in fact, a great part of the object of *dialectic* and *foundations* is to press those very awkward questions which, as a theologian of some particular persuasion, character, and prejudices, one is in the habit of avoiding. Is there or is there not sufficient reason to believe that there is a God, or that God is revealed in Christ? (See Lonergan 1957, chaps. 19 and 20; Lonergan 1972, 101–3). If one rejects religious faith because one rejects all authority, on what consistent principle does one accept authority, as of course we all do, in matters other than religious? Even the most well-educated of contemporary scientists hold most of their scientific beliefs on the authority of other scientists, and the same applies even more strongly to the rest of us (See Lonergan 1957, 703–18).[21] Why does the classical Protestant at once assent to the doctrine of the Trinity as central to the Christian faith and censure the great Scholastics for propounding doctrines and using terminology with no direct Scriptural warrant? (Lonergan 1972, 138). Do Roman Catholics assent to the dogma of Mary's Assumption in accordance with some articulate theological principle, or out of sentiment or group prejudice? (Lonergan 1967, 68–82)

(xii) *Lonergan's distinctions between the basic elements in the cognitional process are too vague to be serviceable* (Corcoran 1975, 60–61, 67, 72). A detailed reply to this charge would take us too far afield. But readers would find it instructive to consider instances in which they have come to know

---

[21] See also Lonergan 1972, 42: "the surveyors believing one another, and the rest of us believing the surveyors."

anything, and to consider whether in doing so they have performed the conscious acts that Lonergan has described. They might then apply his findings to other more controversial cases of actual or alleged knowledge. But, as levelled by the critic herself, the charge does seem to be founded on a misapprehension. Somehow she has managed to persuade herself that Lonergan holds common sense to be the special province of experience, science that of understanding, history that of judgment, and so on. What I think must have misled her is Lonergan's thesis that although *all* four levels of consciousness are applicable to *all* the functional specialties, *research* is in a special way concerned with fixing with relevant data, *interpretation* with understanding them, *history* with judging truly what was going forward, *dialectic* with determining how far what was going forward was right or wrong, and so on (Lonergan 1972, chap. 5). Naturally, this writer found her misapprehension of Lonergan's intention at contradicted time and time again by what he actually said. However, rather than questioning her original interpretation, she concluded that Lonergan's distinctions were too "blurred" to be of use (Corcoran 1975, 67).

Perhaps the best commentary on this criticism is to be found in an article by Lonergan himself:"

> The greater the interpreter's experience, the more cultivated his understanding, the better balanced his judgment, and the more delicate his conscience, the greater will be the likelihood that he will hit upon the meaning intended by the author. . . . The controversialist . . . will assume that his misunderstanding yields a correct interpretation and he will proceed to demonstrate the author's numerous errors and absurdities. But the interpreter will consider the possibility that he himself is at fault. He reads further. Eventually he stumbles upon the possibility that the writer was thinking not of Q but of P, and the meaning of the text becomes plain (Lonergan 1973, 90, 92).

Controversialists may need to evince and justify a dismissive attitude in order to bolster up tender egos, or to curry favor with the members of their group. It would be a pity to spoil the show by a too careful attention to what an author has actually said, or a too intelligent envisagement of the range of that author's possible meaning, or a too reasonable selection of the meaning which appears to fit the evidence best, or a too responsible decision to assert it at all hazards.

Professor Torrance "wanted to know if Lonergan was an old-style Roman Catholic or a new-style Tillich, and he felt that Lonergan's work would not allow him to decide. . . . Could anyone . . . resolve that problem any better than Lonergan did or could?" (Corcoran 1975, 158). But Lonergan himself could, and did. The basic principle to be borne in mind here is that *foundations* select *doctrines* (Lonergan 1972, 132, 142, chaps. 11 and 12); that is, one applies intelligence and reason to the data of the religious tradition, to find out what one is to believe and to disbelieve. The object of theology within these specialties is to ensure that one does so in as thorough and unbiased a manner as possible. The older dogmatics, Protestant as well as Catholic, stressed the objective truth of what is to be believed at the expense of the subject who is supposed to give personal assent to it; against this the pronounced emphasis on the religious subject in theologians like Schleiermacher and Tillich is a reaction. But in so far as one is at all clear about how Lonergan relies on *foundations* to select *doctrines*, the idea of any fundamental conflict between these viewpoints appears quite mistaken. One might just as well challenge biologists to say whether they believe in the hypothetico-deductive method or in the theory of evolution, as though one could not possibly believe in both, and in the latter precisely because of a belief in the former.

# Chapter 4

# FROM METHOD TO THEOLOGY

"Faith is the knowledge born of religious love" (Lonergan 1972, 115). In effect, persons of good will are invited to accept the doctrines of Christianity as meeting their religious feelings, their moral conscience, and their intellectual demands. Of course, it goes without saying that nothing is more common in the modern world than the more or less explicit assumption that rigorous pursuit of truth or of moral ideals is inimical to religious commitment. However, Lonergan has argued at length that this assumption is based either on a misapprehension of the exigencies of intelligence and reason, or on a misunderstanding of the nature of religion.[1]

What in outline is the religious doctrine that the person of good will is invited to accept? Lonergan is a Christian and a Roman Catholic; his answer will be summarised in the next few paragraphs, and set out at greater length in subsequent chapters. What has to be borne in mind throughout is that Lonergan, following Augustine and Aquinas (and incidentally, it is interesting to note, on the same lines as several great Hindu theologians),[2] maintains that the human mind and its operations provides a model in terms of which we can grasp—to some degree, within the limits available to human beings on earth—the meaning of the truths about God revealed through the Bible and the tradition of the Church. This is probably the most important corollary of his insistence that a contemporary theology be grounded in the realm of "interiority."

God is related to all that exists which is other than God much as human conscious subjects are related to their actions and products. There is an unrestricted act of understanding, which understands everything possible, and wills everything actual. Everything else that exists, exists only by virtue of being understood and willed by this being, which is what we call God. There is good reason to believe both that God exists (Lonergan 1957, chap. 19), and that God is revealed in a special way through the message contained in Scripture and entrusted to the Church (Lonergan 1957, chap. 20). God is also known, more or less, through the other great religions of humankind, not only as Creator, but as the infinite love of which human loving is a distant

---

[1] The whole of *Insight* is in essence an argument to this effect; see Lonergan 1957, especially chaps. 1, 18, 19 and 20.

[2] This would certainly apply to Shankhara, Ramanuja, and Madhva.

and pale reflection.[3] It is not the only or even the chief task of systematic theology to argue *that* God exists, and is revealed in the manner just stated. It also and primarily has to achieve some understanding, within the narrow limits possible to human beings on earth, of *what* God has so revealed.

From sustained reflection on Scripture and the tradition of the Church one learns that although there is but one God, there are three beings, distinct by their mutual relations one to another, who are God. This mystery may be understood, indirectly and incompletely (since we do not enjoy the vision of God along with the blessed in heaven) and yet very usefully, through "the psychological analogy"—that is to say, on the model provided by human consciousness and its acts. I may form a conception of myself; I may evince more or less approval or disapproval of myself as so conceived. Now my conception of myself may be more or less accurate, and my approval of myself as so conceived is liable to be more or less appropriate or inappropriate. Similarly, one may suppose that God who is unrestricted understanding eternally forms a conception or "inner word" of God, and evinces infinite love of God as so conceived. However, in contrast with the human case, God's conception of God's self cannot be other than wholly adequate, or God's love in accordance with this conception other than wholly honorable and appropriate.[4] As conceiving, God "begets;" as conception, God is "begotten;" as evincing love, God "spirates;" as love evinced, God is "spirated." As begetting God is Father; as begotten God is Son; as spirating God is Father and Son together;[5] as spirated God is Holy Spirit. So it is that two "processions" yield four "relations," and four "relations" three "Persons."[6] As thus revealed, the Holy Trinity constitutes the ideal of our relations both to ourselves and to each other. However, human relations, unlike those between the Persons of the Trinity, are typically vitiated by inaccurate conceptions and corrupted affections which tend to reinforce one another;[7] since we misrepresent what we hate, and the misrepresentation provides a pretext for greater hatred.

In the Incarnation, God's eternal conception or "inner word" of God's self became a particular historical individual. Since, *pace* the "Nestorians" and the late Professor Geoffrey Lampe (Lampe 1977), it is one and the same who is both the eternal Word of God and this particular man of history, the Word cannot be said to have united himself, however intimately, with *a man*.

---

[3] Since the writing of *Insight,* Lonergan seems to have been at pains to stress this aspect of the matter, perhaps to compensate for what might seem an over-intellectualist approach to the Deity in that work.

[4] See 85–7, 96–7.

[5] It will be seen that Lonergan's systematics supports the Western Church's view that the Spirit proceeds from Father and Son, as against the Eastern view that she proceeds from the Father only.

[6] Cf. pp. 90–94 below.

[7] Cf. pp. 96–7 below. For a very informal account, see Meynell 1976b, 143–51.

Rather, he took on a range of properties by virtue of which he *became* a man, or, in traditional terms, he united himself with *an individual human nature*.[8] We may gain some understanding of how this might be so, again, by attention to the facts of human consciousness. In our own case, the sensitive and emotional consciousness which we seem to share with the higher animals is to be distinguished from the intellectual and rational consciousness peculiar to human beings among earthly creatures. Nevertheless, it is one and the same human individual, you or I, who is conscious of self in these diverse ways. Rather similarly, the incarnation may be understood to consist in one and the same individual who is conscious of himself as the eternal Word of God and as the man Jesus, and who expresses and speaks of the mysteries of God in the actions and words which were constitutive of his human and historical life.[9]

By living, suffering, and dying as a human being among human beings, the eternal Word inaugurates a set of interpersonal relationships of knowledge and love through which the ravages of moral evil in human individuals and societies may progressively be overcome, and through which the eternal bliss of the triune God may come to be shared by human beings in a union which consists of mutual knowledge and love. The image of substitution— one person paying a penalty owed by others—has its place in a symbolic and dramatic understanding of the atonement, where it is corrected by other images. When pressed in the context of a systematic and technical interpretation, however, it can only lead to an immoral or amoral conception of divine justice, as though human beings could properly be punished for crimes without regard to whether they were themselves responsible for them. Rather we are to understand that, through the suffering and humiliation which he takes upon himself, Christ expresses the utmost horror and grief at the affront to God offered by humanity in sin; and that by their association with and devotion to Christ, Christians may share his attitude to sin, have compunction at their own faults, and so progressively become better persons.[10] This effect of Christ's human life is enhanced by the fact that it was shaped as a matter of fact as a "mystery," that is, as a real sequence of events which is such as to appeal to people's emotions and bind their affections in the way that the falsifications of "myth" are prone to do (Lonergan 1957, 724).[11]

As creator and sustainer of the universe, God is in general omnipresent. The supernatural life bestowed by God in Christ consists of an additional special presence of the divine Persons within creation—of the Son, in the

---

[8] See pp. 103–107, 114–17 below.

[9] See pp. 107–111 below.

[10] See chap. 9 below.

[11] Lonergan 1957, 724. This extremely important notion is not much followed up in the later work.

humanity of Christ; of the Holy Spirit, in the new life here and now enjoyed by those who belong to Christ. [12] Lonergan proposes that there is a similar special presence of the Father within creation, in the vision of God possessed by those whose redemption through Christ is complete (Lonergan 1964b, 227). [13]

Still, for all his interest in establishing the content, the rational coherence, and the relevance of the central Christian doctrines, Lonergan by no means overlooks the requirements of what used to be called "natural" or "fundamental" theology. [14] He holds, in fact, that good reasons, which do not explicitly or covertly assume what they set out to establish, can be given for belief in God, in Christianity, and indeed in the authority of the Roman Catholic Church. In order to set out the way of approach to these topics which Lonergan has developed or sketched, it seems suitable to list a number of questions which might be asked by an honest doubter who was seriously concerned, in a Christian or post-Christian *milieu*, about religious matters.

(i) How are we to be fully authentic human subjects—as attentive, intelligent, reasonable, and responsible as possible—in matters of religion? How are we to decide which are the correct religious, or anti-religious, beliefs to hold, and which, if any, are the right religious or anti-religious authorities to follow?

(ii) Should we affirm that God probably or certainly exists, or that God probably or certainly does not exist?

(iii) If we affirm that God exists, should we or should we not affirm in addition that God is specially revealed in Jesus Christ?

(iv) If we affirm that God is specially revealed in Jesus Christ, on what principles can we determine just what this implies, both theoretically and for the conduct of our lives?

(v) What is the place, if any, of ecclesiastical authority in determining what we ought to believe or to do?

(vi) If we think that Christianity is true, what should be our estimate of other religions?

(vii) If we think that the tenets of some Christian denomination ought to be embraced, what are we to make of the other denominations?

It is important to remember that, on Lonergan's account, the principal purpose of argument on these topics would not be that of triumphantly

---

[12] See pp. 97–101 below.

[13] The Father is specially present in creation in the blessed in heaven, as the Son is in the man Jesus, and the Holy Spirit in those who love God.

[14] This is in marked contrast to Barth's repudiation of natural theology. Barth felt that any attempt of this kind would tend to emasculate or even eliminate revelation. Lonergan meets in his own way, what appears to be the valid aspect of Barth's requirement, by insisting that natural theology should always be carried out in the context of *systematics*, so that it is clear that it is the God of religion, and not a mere abstraction, whose existence is supposed to be established.

putting other people in the wrong. The primary issue in religion, as Lonergan repeatedly insists, is conversion, not proof (Lonergan 1972, 338, 340, 350), and conversion is not *in the first instance* the adoption of one particular set of doctrines to the exclusion of all others. According to him, every great religion can have adherents who are more and less converted (Lonergan 1972, 108–12). The typical situation in life for such arguments would be that of Christians (or, *mutatis mutandis*, other believers) finding out for themselves that there was better reason for believing the religious doctrines which they believed than their contradictories. Then politely, calmly, conceding whatever ought to be conceded, yet after all firmly, they would confute those who maintained that these doctrines were false.[15]

Why should the *question* of God ever arise within the human horizon? Lonergan suggests that, in the last analysis, it does so in relation to each of the last three levels of our cognitional activity. We use our intelligence in finding out what is the case about the world, and assume as a matter of course that this is the right way of going about it. Is this an indication that the world has an intelligent ground? We look for sufficient reason in our judgments. Is this a hint that there is a being who provides the sufficient reason for all else that there is?[16] Again, we exert ourselves, at least occasionally, to make responsible decisions, and to act upon them. But is this phenomenon of human responsibility a mere sport in an indifferent or hostile universe, or are we co-operating or failing to co-operate with a moral purpose which underlies the whole cosmic process (Lonergan 1972, 101–3)?[17] These are questions about God, and it is to them that Christianity and the other religions provide answers, whether true or not.

But how can we establish whether it is true or not that there is a God? How can Lonergan persuade himself, or us, that there are grounds for positing "an unrestricted act of understanding," not only as a kind of ideal to be aspired to by the scientist, but as a really existing being? Lonergan does not accept any version of the ontological argument. He admits that even if a clear notion can be obtained of a being who understands all possible worlds, and wills the one that actually exists, the real existence of such a being does not immediately follow (Lonergan 1957, 670–71). However, he argues that if the universe is nothing but what is to be intelligently grasped and reasonably affirmed, it would seem to be intelligible through and through; and God is the intelligence which ultimately accounts for the intelligibility of the world. Theories of knowledge that are less than comprehensively critical tend to conceive of human understanding as an attempt to impose an intelligible structure on a world which is not in itself intelligible. Upon close examina-

---

15 Cf. Lonergan 1974, 225; also Rahner 1978, 359–66.

16 I find Lonergan a little obscure on this point, but hope that I have summarised his gist.

17 It does not seem to me that the phenomenon of responsibility would be a good basis for argument *that* God exists. However, it would be the best starting-point for arguments for the *relevance* of God's existence to the human condition.

tion, however, all attempts to characterise this world, from that of crude realism to the subtleties of phenomenalist "sense-data," or of Kantian "things in themselves" which impinge inscrutably on human sensitivity,[18] dissolve into incoherence. In the long run they all reduce to the paradox that what *is* to be intelligently conceived and reasonably affirmed on the basis of experience, which is what everyone by their practice if not by their precept assumes the real world to be, is *not* what is thus to be intelligently conceived and reasonably affirmed.[19] If this explanation is criticized at as too anthropomorphic, it may be replied that there cannot but be an intimate relation between the human mind on the one hand and the universe and its ground on the other. "For what is the universe and its ground but the objective of man's detached, disinterested, unrestricted desire to know?" (Lonergan 1957, 657).

In a careful and respectful critique of Lonergan, Professor Ronald Hepburn lays emphasis, in Kantian fashion, on the distinction between what is or may be constitutive of the universe itself and what is regulative for our understanding of it (Hepburn 1973). He also remarks that although it is of the essence of scientific investigation to work towards the removal of all opacities in our understanding of the world, it does not follow that there cannot in reality be opacities that can never be so removed. There would be no such opacities if the world were in principle wholly intelligible, as Lonergan affirms. I think that Lonergan would counter by asking Hepburn what conception he has of the world that remains over and above those parts and aspects of it which we now understand. Is it that which can be grasped intelligently and affirmed reasonably, but has not yet been so? If it is, it seems that the world which is not yet known, as well as that which is already known, is intelligible. If not—if there are things and states of affairs which are not to be known by any intelligent grasp and reasonable affirmation—how could we or any other kind of intelligent being ever come to know of their nature or their existence or occurrence? And if we or they could not, is the conception of such "things" or "states of affairs" in the last resort coherent at all?

The concluding chapters of *Insight* make it clear that Lonergan would perfectly agree with Dorothy Emmet that to assent to the existence of an unrestricted act of understanding is one thing and to be a Roman Catholic Christian another, and that to that extent a "jump" is involved between the one and the other (Emmet 1973). He acknowledges as much in his distinction between "general" and "special transcendent knowledge" (Lonergan 1957, chaps. 19 and 20). How does he justify the move from the one to the

[18] It has been fashionable to claim that Kant did not really hold such a position. But see Strawson 1966, 250.

[19] I summarise here what I have argued at some length elsewhere (Meynell 1976a, especially chaps. 1 and 3; Meynell 1982, chap. 3).

other? I will do what I can to summarize the drift of Lonergan's argument here, which involves a lengthy discussion of psychological, social, and ethical theory. There is a moral evil which corrupts human life both individually and socially. This is largely caused by, and always fatally reinforced by, a "flight from insight" which refuses to admit to the wrongs and injustices perpe-trated or condoned by oneself or by the group to which one belongs (Lone-rgan 1957, 199–203; cf. chaps. 6, 7, and 18). What would resolve this universal moral and social problem, given that the human privilege of freedom which gave rise to the problem in the first place is not to be abrogated? The solution could be an overriding hope and a primary loyalty, sufficient to hearten each of us not merely to acknowledge the existence and universal influence of "individual" and "group bias," but to set ourselves to counteract them and their effects in spite of all the anguish attendant on doing so (Lonergan 1957, 696–703; cf. Lonergan 1972, 117).

There is another aspect to the matter. Human beings have a permanent need for "mystery," for a way of relating themselves in feeling as well as in thought to the "known unknown," to all that they know that they do not know. It is this need that has given rise to the great myths of the past, and to the modern political enthusiasms which present so curiously close an anal-ogy to them. Is there any conceivable way in which the human need for mystery might be met, without a sacrifice or compromise of human intel-ligence and reason? The solution would be the occurrence of a real history, which met the human needs which have given rise to the falsifications of myth (Lonergan 1957, 531–49, 723–24).[20] Given the existence of an infinite understanding and omnipotent will responsible for the universe, one might expect a solution along these lines, and if we survey nature and history, we find that such a solution has been provided. It remains for each human being to embrace the solution, to apply it, and to proclaim it to others.

If such a solution has really been provided, there is the task not only of identifying and living it, but of setting out clearly and distinctly what it consists in and implies both from a theoretical and from a practical point of view. Dorothy Emmet reproaches Lonergan for effectively abandoning the best elements in his theory of knowledge when it comes to religious doctrine (Emmet 1973, 15–16). Lonergan might answer that there is on the contrary a close correspondence between the advance of natural science and the ad-vance of theology as he conceives them. In science, one moves from mere description of phenomena to explanation of them, testing one's theoretical explanations by observation and experiment. Similarly, in theology, there has been the movement from the direct response of the biblical authors to revelatory events, through the preliminary *ad hoc* use of theoretical terms to

[20] It is through meeting this need for "mystery" that the central doctrines of Christianity are, on Lonergan's account, existentially relevant.

meet difficulties which one finds in the Councils from Nicea onwards, to the thoroughgoing theoretical recasting of the content of Christian belief which was the achievement of the great medieval scholastics.

The pronouncements of the *magisterium* are quite closely analogous to crucial experiments in science. They ensure that theology should progress over the course of time, and not simply oscillate between biblical fundamentalism and unbridled speculation—as might not implausibly be said to be the more or less inevitable fate of those kinds of Christian theology which do not acknowledge any such authority. It should be added that there seems no good reason why this kind of theology should not be perfectly compatible with reflection on the riches of one's mystical tradition as commended by Dorothy Emmet (Emmet 1973, 15). Indeed, many of the most notable Christian mystics have had at the center of their devotional life meditation on the mysteries of the Trinity and the Incarnation. On Lonergan's account, the primary function of the *magisterium* is to determine, amidst all the changes and developments of human culture, what does belong to the content of faith, what does not, and what is incompatible with it.[21]

Lonergan does not regard his commitment to Roman Catholic Christianity as implying a negative or dismissive attitude towards other religions. He maintains that God bestows the gift of love in and through all the great religions and religious traditions. Hindus, Muslims, and Buddhists, as well as Christians, can be religiously, morally, and intellectually converted, and can submit to or strive against individual and group bias. Lonergan follows F. Heiler in distinguishing a number of features common to authentic religion, to each of which, he adds, there corresponds an inauthentic perversion (Lonergan 1972, 109; Heiler 1959).[22] "Genuine religion is discovered and realized by redemption from the many traps of religious aberration" (Lonergan 1972, 110). Thus the love of God may easily degenerate into the erotic and orgiastic, and awe of God into a conception of God as remote and irrelevant. The disciplines of prayer and asceticism may come to be ends in themselves rather than means to communion with God. It is perhaps worth noting that such a positive attitude to non-Christian religions does *not* imply that all religions are equally "true," or that it is impossible to believe sincerely but falsely.

I shall conclude the chapter with some suggestions about how Lonergan's method may be applied to the characteristic themes of some of the great Christian theologians of the past. Analysis of the merits and limitations of past theologians is the special task of *dialectic*, the fourth functional spe-

---

[21] This view of the *magisterium* seems presupposed throughout the Latin treatises. See also Lonergan 1972, 327.

[22] I myself believe that Heiler rather exaggerates the unity between the higher religions, but do not think that the use to which Lonergan puts his ideas is vitiated by this. Cf. also Lonergan 1985, 55–73.

cialty, which Lonergan proposes as the ecumenical equivalent of the older polemical or controversial theology.

Luther emphasised superbly the crucial importance of the individual believer's direct apprehension of Christ in faith, and deplored the technical theological subtleties which seemed to deny or to compromise this apprehension. But perhaps he was not perfectly clear about whether this hostility was or ought to have been aimed at systematic theology as such, with its necessary use of non-biblical terms, or at an abuse of it which stifled or misrepresented the essence of the Christian faith. Later Lutheran "scholastics," whose aim was to work out the full consequences of Luther's initial insights, were compelled to resort, as the Nicene Fathers had done over a millennium before, to the use of terms without direct biblical warrant.

The error of what is called "fundamentalism" would seem to be that it is apt to treat the language of the "symbolic construct" (Lonergan 1972, 306) presented in Scripture as though it presupposed the conceptual exactitude and rigor proper to the language of theory.[23] Biblical language directly engages one's emotion and the springs of one's action, whereas the language of theory addresses itself in the first instance only to the intellect. (The language of religious theory is not suitable for to worship and devotion, but it does serve to prevent aberrations of worship and devotion.) Unless this difference is borne in mind, the doctrines of the Trinity and of the divinity of Christ will appear to be founded not on the New Testament witness as a whole, but on a very few isolated texts, at least one of which, the notorious Johannine Comma, is certainly spurious (1 John 5: 7–9). It is perhaps not surprising that the Socinians, in the period after the Reformation, combined a biblical literalism with disbelief in the Trinity and the divinity of Christ. But an effective and irenical *dialectic* should recognize the merit of "fundamentalism" in asserting, in however erroneous a fashion, the inspiration of Scripture against those who seem to deny it explicitly or by implication.

Lonergan's method also discloses—this may be inferred more directly from *Method in Theology* than may my treatment of the previous examples— the characteristic vices of the older Roman Catholic dogmatic theology, which is now out of fashion. The ossification and intransigence of much Scholastic theology is due to neglect of the fact, clearly demonstrated by

---

[23] Of course, *that* any writing or set of writings is to be accepted as "Scripture" in this sense is a "doctrine" to be established, or refuted, by application of the second, third, fourth, fifth, and sixth functional specialties to the data relevant to religion. Very briefly and roughly, as Lonergan sees it, there are reasons for thinking that God exists (see Lonergan 1957, chap. 19 and pp. 51–53 above), that God has provided a solution to the problem of human wrongdoing, and that there is a community which has the task of promulgating and implementing that solution (see Lonergan 1957, chap. 20, and 94–96; Meynell 1976a, chaps. 6 and 7). The Bible expresses the community's apprehension of that solution at an early and crucial stage of its development (see p. 22 above).

Lonergan's method, that the same dogma can be expressed in many different ways and from many different points of view. On the other hand, the sentimentality and confusion attributable to much liberal Protestant theology seems largely due to oversight of the fact that many formulations are such that they really weaken, compromise, or deny the essentials of faith. Lonergan's method issues in principles whose application tends to correct both abuses.

I understand that T. F. Torrance has referred to Lonergan as "the Catholic Schleiermacher." The comparison is a profound and useful one, in that both Schleiermacher and Lonergan are preoccupied with the human subject and his consciousness. But Lonergan's emphasis on the importance of *doctrines* and *systematics,* as well as of *foundations*—the articulation of the "horizon" of the conscious subject, that is to say, of his consciousness and the main lines of what he can come to know—shows that he is by no means neglectful of the divine Object of theological discourse.[24] Even if it can be plausibly said that Schleiermacher's theology reduces in the last analysis to religious talk about oneself, the same is certainly not true of Lonergan's. It might well be claimed, indeed, that Lonergan has at last provided the much-needed synthesis between the points of view of Schleiermacher and Barth. To Barth's polemic against "natural theology," Lonergan would reply in effect that the fact that "philosophy of God" is no *substitute* for theology does not entail that it is *dispensable,*[25] and that Christian doctrine can be shown to meet human aspirations which do not presuppose its truth (Lonergan 1957, chap. 20). If Barth were to object that this is unduly to exalt humanity in the face of God's gracious revelation, Lonergan would answer that the authentic human being's reaching towards God is itself the result of God's gift of love (Lonergan 1972, 340–41).[26] It is under the influence of the Holy Spirit that human persons who have not previously believed in God or in Christ may ask whether they may reasonably and responsibly do so; and *foundations* applied to the fruit of *dialectic* and issuing in *doctrines* give them their answer. Incidentally, in his account of *dialectic* and *foundations,* and particularly of what he calls "intellectual conversion," Lonergan has provided a powerful and convincing counterblast to those analytic philosophers who contest the meaningfulness of Christian belief on epistemological grounds. Briefly and crudely, the claim that God is not to be known in just the way that a physical object present here and now to one's senses might be supposed to be known does not imply that God is not to be known at all.

On the matter of inter-religious and inter-donominational dialogue, it is to be noted that Lonergan follows Wilfred Cantwell Smith in distinguishing

[24] One the senses in which God is and is not an object, see Lonergan 1972, 341–42; 1974, 121–27.

[25] See Lonergan 1973a; also n. 14 above.

[26] Lonergan cites the remark which Pascal attributes to God, "You would not be seeking me if you had not already found me" (*Pensées,* vii, 553).

"faith," as the direct result of God's gift of love, from the "beliefs" in which it is expressed in the different religions and denominations. He makes this distinction because he admits that one may be in love with God without accurate knowledge of God, or even, in some cases, without acknowledging God's existence at all. However, among the values which "faith" is apt to discern is that of accepting the judgments of fact and value, the "beliefs," proposed by a religion (Lonergan 1972, 118). Lonergan remarks that the distinction between "faith" and "beliefs" provides a basis for ecumenical discussion. There is good reason to suppose that if God wills all persons to be saved (1 Tim. 2:4), the authentic adherents of every religion have received God's gift of love (Lonergan 1972, 119). He is aware that this claim brings him into apparent conflict with an older and more authoritative Catholic tradition which identifies faith with beliefs. But he suggests that his departure is rather from the older way of speaking than from the substance of the older claim. Where Lonergan speaks of a "faith" that grounds "beliefs," the older way of speaking would have a *lumen gratiae* or infused wisdom which grounds "faith" (Lonergan 1972, 123).

I have sketched Lonergan's approach to the questions of why it is reasonable and responsible to believe in God and in Christ, and to accept the special office of the Catholic Church in promulgating doctrine. It is important to remember that the existence of God, the divinity of Christ, and the special office of the Catholic Church, are *doctrines* which, according to Lonergan, may be vindicated by *applying* the method. They are not *presupposed* by the method itself, which may be employed by persons of sufficient intelligence and good will whatever religion they belong to, and indeed whether they belong to any religion or not. Catholic faith, and indeed the faith of most non-Catholic Christians, includes assent to the truth of certain doctrines, in particular those of the Trinity, the Incarnation, and the Atonement. What do these doctrines mean and imply, how are they based on Scripture, and how are they relevant to the human condition? By what steps have they been progressively developed by the reflections of theologians and the pronouncements of the *magisterium?* Lonergan's arguments and conclusions on these matters will be summarised in the remaining chapters.[27]

[27] On the alleged existential irrelevance of theological systematics, see p. 24 above. One might comment that, while cytological and pharmacological research are not directly involved in the treatment of patients in hospitals, it will hardly be denied that they are of great though indirect relevance to such treatment. Similarly, the working-out of the detailed consequences of the doctrines of Christ's divinity and humanity, and the demonstration that they are consistent with one another, is not of direct significance for the religious devotion of ordinary people. But that Jesus is both God and man is certainly so relevant and the consequences of this belief, as worked out by the systematic theologian, are therefore indirectly so.

# Chapter 5

# THE DIVINITY OF THE SON AND OF THE HOLY SPIRIT

It is obvious enough that Christ is actually said to be God in very few texts of the New Testament. How, if at all, then, can it be argued, as it has been by Christian theologians at large, that the doctrine of his divinity is founded in Scripture?

First, a little must be said about the conception of God presupposed in the New Testament. It is summed up in the phrase "the God of Abraham, the God of Isaac, the God of Jacob, the God of our fathers." As the phrase implies, this conception was evolved in response to historical events, and was transmitted through the medium of traditional narratives. For the New Testament writers, God was in the first instance *the one who* had had dealings with the Patriarchs, *the one who* had led Israel out of Egypt through the agency of Moses, *the one who* raised up prophets to teach and correct them, and so on. The first important development in this concept came about when the Gospel was preached to the Gentiles, as may be inferred from a comparison of the speeches of Paul to the Jews and Gentiles reported in *Acts*.[1] The transition involved is from a historically-mediated conception to one derived from general reflection on the world. Although the Gentiles lacked the particular traditions characteristic of Jewish culture, they could be told about a God supposed to be cause of the world as a whole. Lonergan remarks rather wrily that it is misunderstanding of the nature of this transition which has given rise to that well-known and exceedingly misleading antithesis between the God of Abraham, Isaac, and Jacob on the one hand and the God of the philosophers on the other (Lonergan 1964c, 18–19).

The second important development, which will have to be described at some length, is that by which terms signifying attributes of God, and the term "God" itself, gradually became applied to the Son and the Holy Spirit as well as to the Father.

It might be asked why the revelation of the divinity of Christ in Scripture could not have been more direct, assuming that it happened at all. Lonergan points out that one has to take into account the nature of the religious development which was taking place. Christ founded not a school, but a Church, and the first requirement was that people should be converted. The

---

[1] Acts 13:16–22; 14:15–17; 17:24–28.

progressive revelation of the divinity of Jesus Christ was but one aspect of a process in which people were being transformed into new creatures.[2] Again, one must remember that every successful instance of teaching must begin from the pupil's prior state of knowledge. Thus infants, children, uneducated adults, and educated adults must be taught in different ways, and differences due to the place and time in which people live, and the general state of culture which prevails in their environment must also to be taken into account. Lonergan imagines a very green theological student asking why Jesus could not just have stood up among the Jews and said, "I am God, in a strict sense," and saved the later church a great deal of trouble. The answer is, first, that what was meant by "God" in that milieu was what was later meant by "God the Father," and Jesus is not God the Father. Again, the expression "strictly speaking" presupposes a kind of sophistication and precision in the use of concepts such as had not developed at that place and time. Christianity was new, and it was new in one way to Jews, and in another way to Gentiles. Thus such terms as were available had to be put to a new use and understood in a new way (Lonergan 1964c, 22–23).

A grasp of the nature and necessity of such development is an effective remedy, as Lonergan sees it, against two recurrent and antithetical dangers of interpretation. The first is the anachronism which attributes to an earlier age what belongs only to a later one, and the second the archaism which insists on earlier conceptions and modes of expression to such an extent as to preclude valid later developments. Thus anachronism finds the doctrine defined by the Council of Chalcedon, that there are one Person and two natures in Christ, everywhere in the New Testament. Of course, this makes argument from Scripture for the divinity of Christ very easy. But unfortunately it does so at the cost of falsifying the original meaning of the relevant texts as intended by their authors. This error inevitably brings forth its opposite, the archaism which insists on the concepts and terminology of the New Testament in such a way that conciliar decrees are repudiated as contrary to Scripture. But it is just the same error that vitiates both attitudes. This is, both overlook the fact that what is at bottom one and the same teaching may over the course of time be grasped from a series of different viewpoints, and be expressed in terms of conceptions which evolve in accordance with these (Lonergan 1964c, 24–27; 1972, 312).

The unique sense in which Jesus is claimed to be God's "Son" appears in the distinction implied throughout the New Testament, with various degree of emphasis, between the one who redeems and those who are to be redeemed. In the Synoptic Gospels, Jesus is God's "beloved Son," and others are commanded to listen to him. Again, according to the Synoptics, Jesus speaks of "my Father" and "your Father," but he is never represented

---

[2] Cf. 2 Cor. 5:17.

as saying "*our* Father," except in a context where he is telling his *disciples* how they ought to pray.[3] St. Paul uses what amounts to a technical term, *huiothesia,* to distinguish the sonship of the faithful from that of Christ.[4] In the Gospel of John, Jesus is "the only-begotten Son," and the faithful are called not "sons" *(huioi)* but "children" *(tekna)* of God.[5] It is notable that in one place a quotation from the Psalms is broken off, apparently in order to avoid infringing this rule. Jesus quotes the text, "I said, you are gods," but does not continue, "and all sons *(huioi)* of the Highest."[6] The special sense in which Christ is the Son of God is compendiously expressed at the beginning of the Epistle to the Hebrews. The Son is he whom God "has made heir to the whole universe, and through whom he created all orders of existence; . . . the effulgence of God's splendor and the stamp of God's very being."[7] Both Christ and his followers are said to be filled with God or inhabited by God. Yet there is a difference in the mode of habitation, which is in the hearts of believers by faith, but in Christ "bodily" *(somatikōs).*[8] the uniqueness of the relationship is brought out also by those so-called "trinitarian" texts which mention Father, Son and Holy Spirit together. Again, reconciliation with the Father is *through* the Son; and the Spirit which is given to believers, whereby they are made sons in their turn, is the Spirit *of* the Son.[9]

It may be asked in what sense, if at all, the doctrine that the Son is "consubstantial" with the Father is adumbrated in Scripture. Now the Son is consubstantial with the Father if and only if what is true of the Father is also true of the Son. And this, according to Lonergan, is implied or hinted at in many places. The Father and the Son are said to have mutual and exclusive knowledge one of the other.[10] The title *kurios* ("Lord") is ascribed in the Greek version of the Old Testament to God, and in the New Testament to Christ. Thus "the day of the Lord" announced by the prophets[11] comes to be understood by the New Testament writers as the day of Jesus Christ.[12] Similarly the prophetic preparation of the way of the Lord becomes the preparation of the way of Christ.[13] Doxologies formerly addressed to God only become addressed to Christ.[14] The title "King of Kings and Lord of

---

[3] Mark 1:11, 9:7 and parallels; Matt. 6:9.

[4] Gal. 4:5; Rom. 8:15, 9:4; Eph. 1:5.

[5] John 1:12; 11:52.

[6] John 10:34; cf. Ps. 82:6.

[7] Heb. 1:2–3.

[8] Col. 2:9.

[9] Gal. 4:6.

[10] Matt. 11:27; Luke 10:22.

[11] E.g. Joel 3:4, cited Acts 2:20.

[12] 1 Cor. 1:8; 2 Cor. 1:14; 2 Thess. 2:1–2.

[13] Mal. 3:1; Mark 1:2.

[14] Heb. 13:21; 1 Pet. 4:11; Rev. 5:12–13.

Lords," ascribed to God in the Old Testament, is ascribed to "the Lamb" (Christ) in the Book of Revelation.[15] The affirmation "I am," uttered by God in the Old Testament in particularly solemn contexts, is uttered similarly by Christ in the Gospel of John.[16] The titles "Alpha and Omega," "first and last," "beginning and end," are applied by the Book of Revelation both to God and to Christ.[17] Father and Son are associated in the work of creation. All things are said to be related to God the Father as him *from* whom, and to the Lord Jesus Christ as him *in* whom, they are. Things are said to be created *in* as well as *through* the Son; the Son is said to sustain everything by his word of power; and God is said to have created the ages through him. In the Gospel of John it is not only asserted that the Word is that through which the world was made, but it is stated in so many words that nothing was made without him.[18] And, of course, Christ is actually called God in a few texts—[19] which ought to be mentioned, even though it would be utterly mistaken to regard them as the sole and sufficient Scriptural basis for the doctrine of Christ's divinity (Lonergan 1964a, 113–4; 1964c 52, 61).

The term "Word," as applied to the Son in the Prologue to the Fourth Gospel, deserves special attention in this connection.[20] Lonergan suggests that the eternal and the temporal are compared and contrasted in a number of ways in this passage, notably by means of antithesis between the verbs *einai* (to be) and *gignesthai* (to become), which not only occur repeatedly, but make up a kind of antiphonal chant. "In the beginning *was* (ēn) the Word; "There *appeared (egeneto)* a man;" "That *was* (ēn) the true light;" "And the Word *became (egeneto)* flesh;" "he *being* (ōn) in the bosom of the Father."[21] The saying of Jesus later in the Gospel may be compared: "Before Abraham came into being, I am" *(prin Abraam genesthai ego eimi)*.[22] Lonergan suggests that a threefold distinction is being made. First, the Word spoken of by John was not made, did not come into being, but simply was. Second, the Word was not just *of* the Lord or *of* God, like the prophetic word of the Old Testament, but actually God.[23] Third, while the prophetic word is a word spoken or given *to* someone, the Word described by John is *with* God, and was *with* him from the beginning.[24] It cannot be that the Word was made, and is therefore a creature, since without the Word nothing was made.[25] The

---

[15] Deut. 10:17; Dan. 2:47; Rev. 17:14.
[16] Exod. 3:14; Isa. 43:10; John 8:24, 28, 58; 13:19.
[17] Rev. 1:8, 17; 2:8; 21:6; 22:13.
[18] 1 Cor. 8:6; Col. 1:16; Heb. 1:2–3; John 1:3, 10.
[19] 2 Pet. 1:1; Tit. 2:13; Heb. 1:9; John 20:28; 1 John 5:20.
[20] John 1:1–14.
[21] John 1:1, 9, 14, 18.
[22] John 8:58.
[23] John 1:1.
[24] John 1:1–2.
[25] John 1:3.

Word gives and sends the Spirit, [26] and is therefore distinct from the word which was given *by* the Spirit to the prophets (Lonergan 1964c, 49–50, 52–61; 1964a, 113–14, 124–25, 127).

What is the significance of the term "word"? There is no need to pause over the literal sense, which points to a spoken word which may be heard and a written word which may be seen. In a transferred sense, a "word" is a meaning manifested in speech, or the intellectual and rational principle in persons which they express in "words" in the literal sense, and by which they seek, discover, and propound the reasons for things. In yet another sense, the "word" may be understood as that within things by virtue of which they may be known through the exercise of intelligence and reason. [27] It was in this sense that the Stoics postulated a "word" immanent in things themselves, and the Neoplatonists a "word" which was such as to transcend the sensible world, being identical with the intelligible realm of ideas. Ancient pagan divinities like Hermes, Isis, Thoth, and so on came to be understood as cosmological principles, and were thus called "words" in a rather similar sense. Philo of Alexandria identified the "word" of the Platonists with the idea of the world in the mind of the Creator, and he named this idea the Word of God. [28] In the Old Testament, among other senses of "the Word of God," there stand out particularly the creative Word and the prophetic Word. The word of God is sometimes personified, [29] in much the same way as is the wisdom of God. [30] In the New Testament "the word of God" usually means the gospel, in the sense of the content of the Church's preaching. [31] The Johannine Word is distinct from yet related to all of these. Lonergan suggests that in the same sense in which Paul said there were many (so-called) gods and lords, [32] so John might have said that there are many so-called words. The Word proclaimed by John is related to the Stoic word as cause to effect, to the Platonic word as personal to impersonal principle, to the word of pagan religions as the true to the false (Lonergan 1964c, 75–84).

A later passage in the Fourth Gospel is about the equality of Jesus with God. [33] In considering this passage, Lonergan proposes that one attend to the *ground* of the accusation by the Jews that Jesus is making himself the equal of God, to the *accusation itself,* and to the *response* given by Jesus to the accusation. In all three instances, equality of some kind is at issue, but the

---

[26] John 15:26; 16:14, 15.

[27] That the real is what is to be known by the application of intelligence and reason to the data of the senses is, of course, a cardinal principle of Lonergan's thought. Cf. pp. 1–7 above.

[28] Philo, *De Opif, Mundi*, 24.

[29] Isa. 55:10–11; Wis. 18:14–16.

[30] Wis. 7:22, 25, 27; Prov. 8:22–36.

[31] 1 Thess. 2:13, Eph. 1:13, etc.

[32] 1 Cor. 8:5.

[33] John 5:16–30.

force of the passage as a whole depends on a contrast between kinds and degrees of equality. For while there is some ground for the accusation in what has preceded it, there is much more in the reply given by Jesus. Not only do Jesus' words[34] fail to remove the original ground of the accusation, that he works on the sabbath just as the Father does.[35] They increase it to a staggering degree. The passage calls attention to those very attributes which Jews considered peculiar to God, and applies them to the Son, who is said to do what the Father does,[36] to bring the dead to life like the Father,[37] to be judge of human beings in the Father's place,[38] and to be worthy of the same honor as the Father.[39] Each one of these claims, as Lonergan says, to say nothing of the sum of them taken together, far exceeds the grounds of the original accusation. Of course it would be anachronistic to state the evangelist's meaning in the technical terminology which evolved later. The notion of "equality" which is at issue in this passage is evidently a somewhat open one which can be further determined, and indeed almost demands to be so. Lonergan suggests that the passage as a whole provides a good example of the manner in which Scripture, proceeding as it does from the inspiration of the Holy Spirit, prepares for and aims at the evolution of doctrines which was later to take place (Lonergan 1964c, 91–93).[40]

In the New Testament, as Lonergan points out, is found a kind of twofold variation in the use of terms applied to God the Father and to Jesus. When God the Father is simply "God," Jesus is apt to be referred to as "Son of Man" or "Son of God." Where "God the Father" is named as such, Jesus is usually called "Son of the Father" or "his Son." Thus in John the term "the Son" is often used without addition or qualification in reference to Jesus[41]—a use which is rare in the Synoptics[42] and Paul. Lonergan makes in this connection the general point that in such cases as this linguistic usage changes only step by step, since otherwise a new usage is not understood. In

---

[34] Ibid., 19–30.

[35] Ibid., 16–18.

[36] Ibid., 19.

[37] Ibid., 21.

[38] Ibid., 22.

[39] Ibid., 23.

[40] An objection to the Son's equality with the Father might be based on the Son's statement that the Father is greater than himself (John 14:28). In the technical terms worked out by the medieval Scholastic theologians, the answer might be given that the Father is greater than the Son both in that his divinity is greater than the Son's humanity, and in that he who confers divinity is greater than him who receives it; but that the Father is not greater in having a greater divinity, since the divine substance is one in Father and Son. In the terms used in the Fourth Gospel itself, the Father is greater than the Son in that the Son can do nothing of himself (John 5:19, 30), derives the life that is within him from the Father (5:26), and receives from the Father the teaching which he gives (8:28). But this is perfectly consistent with the kind of equality with the Father which is also claimed (Lonergan 1964c, 100).

[41] John 3:35, 36' 5:19–23, 26; 6:40; etc.

[42] Matt. 11:27, 24:36; 28:19; Mark 13:32; Luke 10:22.

the New Testament the term denoting the First Person of the Trinity seems to change gradually from "God" to "the Father," as though to hint that another divine Person is being revealed, the Son (Lonergan 1964a, 121–22).

The New Testament texts which have the most immediate bearing on the divinity of Christ may be divided into two main groups. Those of the first group employ honorific terms and titles of the sort which were already current in the Palestinian milieu at the time of Jesus, and could be adapted to express his special status. Those of the second group, which are to be found especially in the Epistles and in the Fourth Gospel, employ what might be called quasi-theological terms. To call them "theological" is not to deny that they belong to the divine revelation upon which it is the task of theology to reflect, but rather to bring out their resemblance, in their almost technical use of terms, to theology properly speaking. What is implied by the titles employed in the former group of texts is clarified by the conceptions characteristic of the second, and what may seem dubious or ambiguous in the conceptions is corroborated and rendered more concrete by the titles. Thus each part of the material illuminates and confirms the rest. Lonergan suggests that just as the organs of an animal or plant are connected and related to one another in innumerable ways, so in that spiritual organism which is the New Testament there is a full, firm and subtle interdependence and interpenetration of the constituent elements (Lonergan 1964c, 44–45).

The early Fathers accepted the preaching of the apostles as their rule of faith. According to Irenaeus, the Church, though scattered through the world, speaks with one voice by virtue of its acceptance of the apostolic preaching.[43] Tertullian uses precisely the same criterion for detecting and repudiating heresy.[44] Both make a clear distinction between what is subject to this rule of faith and what is their own private judgment. In the writings of Clement of Alexandria and Origen, the distinction is made quite systematically between the common rule of faith on the one hand and the knowledge which a person may obtain by a diligent study of Scripture on the other.[45] It was by the same principle—conformity with what was supposed to have been taught by and handed faithfully down from the apostles—that the canon of Scripture was determined and that heretics were excluded from the Church (Lonergan 1964a, 128–30).

Lonergan points out that there is pagan and heretical witness to the fact that the Christians neither tolerated a plurality of gods in the manner of the pagans nor admitted like the Jews that there was only one who was God. In his letter to the emperor Trajan, the younger Pliny describes the Christians in his province as meeting and singing hymns to Christ as though to a god.[46] Lucian says that the Christians have rejected the gods of the Greeks, and

---

[43] *Adv. Haer.*, I, 10, 2.
[44] *De praescr. haeret.*, 21.
[45] Cf. Origen, *De princ.*, praef. 3.
[46] *Ad Traianum epist.*, X, 96, 7.

"adore their crucified sophist and order their lives according to his law."[47]
Origen quotes Celsus as saying that the Christians would perhaps have right
on their side if they worshipped simply the one God, but that where they
went wrong was in worshipping a man of recent times, the leader of their
sedition, and claiming him to be the unique son of God.[48] This mysterious
account of God, which somehow asserted of God both singularity and multiplicity, inevitably gave rise to a whole series of interpretations. Thus the
Jewish Ebionites and the Greek Adoptionists maintained that Jesus was
simply a man with a unique mission, the Gnostics and Marcionites that the
severe Creator God of the Old Testament was a different being from the
merciful God of the New, the Patripassians that the Father who created and
the Son who redeemed were absolutely one and the same, while the
Sabellians distinguished three names as denoting three activities of one and
the same being. All these positions were rejected by the Church, yet the
Church itself only came step by step to a more or less adequate formulation
of its belief on the matter (Lonergan 1964a, 132–34).

It is something of a cliché, and true within certain limits, that the Fathers
were influenced by Greek metaphysics in their expression of Christian
belief. Without doubt, both Stoicism and Neoplatonism strongly affected the
manner in which the ante-Nicene Fathers understood the relations between
God the Father and Christ. However, as Lonergan argues often and at length
(Lonergan 1976a, sections 6, 10), they did not affect the doctrine of the Son's
consubstantiality with the Father as defined at the Council of Nicea. It is
sometimes claimed that the ante-Nicene Fathers were "subordinationist",[49]
but the term is apt to cause confusion in this context, presupposing as it does
distinctions which had not yet been made. It is better to say that their
manner of expression serves to show that they effectively acknowledged the
divinity of the Son, without actually excluding subordinationism.

The view which seems to have been usual among these authors is set out
with particular clarity by Tertullian. The somewhat materialistic manner in
which Tertullian conceives the unity of Father and Son is due partly to the
influence of Stoicism and partly to the fact that no alternative was available
until the necessary differentiation of consciousness had been achieved.[50] The
Word of God, he says, is not empty and insubstantial like the word from the
lips of a man. It is itself a substance, proceeding as it does from so great a
substance, and being itself creator of such great substances.[51] God utters the
Word as the root puts forth the plant, the source the stream, and the sun its
radiance. As the plant cannot be separate from its root, or the stream from its
source, or its radiance from the sun, no more can his Word be sundered from

[47] *Peregrinus*, 11 and 13.
[48] *C Celsum*, VIII 12, VIII 14.
[49] Subordinationism is the heretical view that the Son is subordinate to the Father, or the
Holy Spirit to the Father and the Son.
[50] See pp. 29–30, 34–38 above.
[51] *Adv. Prax.*, 7.

God.[52] And he says much the same thing about the relation of the Holy Spirit to the Father and the Son (Lonergan 1964a, 45–47).

The difference between Tertullian's conception of the unity between Father and Son and that of Athanasius, which was so crucial for subsequent developments, was as follows. Both were in effect trying to expound what amounted to the same belief—that the Father is God, and the Son is God, and the Father is not the Son, and yet that there is only one God. Both provide imaginative analogies by which this position can to some extent be grasped. Athanasius, however, also propounds his epoch-making rule, that the same things are to be said of the Son as of the Father, except only that the Son is not the Father. Tertullian, by contrast, remains at a sensory and materialistic level of conception. He conceives the spiritual as if it were merely a specially tenuous kind of material, and envisages the unity of substance (as it later came to be termed) in God in terms of a kind of physical continuity (Lonergan 1964a, 48; 1976a, 47).

Now it is characteristic of dialectic, as it may be called, that it arises from some contradiction, and heads towards the elimination of that contradiction.[53] In the development of Christian theology, where a matter of central significance is at stake, the final result of such dialectic is either explicit heresy or an advance in doctrine. When the contradiction is only latent, dialectic makes it explicit, and it becomes clear that one cannot assert at one and the same time the contradictory propositions involved. The more difficult the question at issue, and the more sluggish the intellectual processes of those who are thinking about them, the more slowly is the latent contradiction brought to light. Lonergan points out that the working of the dialectical process is generally to be seen most clearly in the work not of a single author, but of a series of authors, each of whom contributes something towards the ultimate clarification and resolution of the issue. In the case being considered here, the latent contradiction is exemplified in Tertullian. He taught that the Father and the Son were both one God, and yet distinct from one another. At the same time, he held that the Son was a temporal being, and that the divine substance as a whole was to be distinguished from some portion or derivative of it. Arius from his point of view, and Athanasius from his, were to make absolutely clear what later theologians came to take for granted, that the Son must be creator or creature, but cannot be something somehow in between (Lonergan 1964a, 49–50, 59; 1976a, 48–49).

Whereas Tertullian used material analogies to explain the unity of substance between Father and Son, Origen resorted to conceptions derived from Platonism. Thus he rejected as unsuitable any comparison with human or animal generation,[54] or with the kind of physical division into parts that one finds in Tertullian. More positively, he maintains that the Son is God in

---

[52] Ibid., 8.

[53] This is not of course identical with the functional specialty *dialectic*; for all that the latter is concerned with the former.

[54] *De princ.*, I, 2, 5; I, 2, 6.

that he contemplates the depths of the Father, but Son in that he continually embraces the Father's will.[55] And he proposes a specifically psychological theory of their unity: the Son proceeds from the Father, as a human act of will proceeds from a human mind (Lonergan 1976a, 60). However, some of his speculations seem less fortunate, at least in the light of later developments. Thus he held that whereas the Father was God in himself *(autotheos)*, the Son was God by participation *(metoche)*,[56] and that whereas the Son is good, the Father is good beyond all comparison, goodness itself.[57] Obviously these views are founded on a Platonic theory of participation.[58] Similarly he maintains that whereas Christ is true light and true life, the Father of light and life is greater.[59] He interprets in a very radical fashion the text "The Father is greater than I;"[60] while the Son and Holy Spirit far excel all other beings, he claims, the Father in turn excels the Son and the Spirit by as much or even more (Lonergan 1964a, 55–58; 1976a, sec. VII).[61]

Now if the Son is God in virtue of consisting of some of the same quasi-material stuff as God the Father, it does not appear in the least incompatible with his divinity if he comes into being in time, by the free choice of the Father, for the purpose of creating and governing the world. However, if the Son's divinity is conceived not in this uncritical manner, but as implying that what is true of the Father is true of the Son, such a conception of the Son's origin is clearly ruled out. For if this principle is adhered to, one denies the

[55] *In Ioan.*, II, 2 (Migne 1866 [MG in subsequent references] 14, 110B). Ibid. XIII, 36 (MG 14, 461C).

[56] *In Ioan.*, II, 2 (MG 14, 110 AB).

[57] *De Princ.*, I, 2, 13 (MG 11, 143C).

[58] According to this theory, for instance, all circular things participate in the subsistent form of the circular, all blue things participate in the subsistent form of the blue.

[59] *In Ioan.*, II, 23 (MG 14, 156A); XIII, 3 (MG 14, 404C).

[60] John 14:28.

[61] *In Ioan.*, XIII, 25 (MG 14, 411 B). It may be asked how far Origen can be claimed as a predecessor of the Arians, as they themselves maintained that he was. It must be remembered that Origen was more of a Scriptural exegete than a philosopher or metaphysician in the strict sense, and thought in concrete and dynamic terms rather than with the logical precision attained by later theologians. He did not see what became clear to his successors, that one being could not at once be creature and Creator. The question is whether Origen in effect believed that the Son is a creature. There is no doubt that he occasionally asserted this in so many words, as indeed others did, on the understanding that the following text of Scripture referred to the Son: "The Lord created me at the beginning of his works, before all else that he made, long ago" (Prov. 8:22; *De Princ.*, IV, 4, 1). However, Origen also taught that the Son was strictly speaking eternal, and denied that he had ever come into existence, or that there was a time when he did not exist (*C. Celsum*, IV, 17; *In Ioan*, fragm. 2; *De Princ.*, IV, 4, 1). Given the clarity of the issue as later set out by Athanasius, that the Son is *either* consubstantial with the Father *or* a creature, but cannot be both or neither, then some remarks of Origen are inconsistent with the Son's divinity. But one must not confuse such a conclusion with views which Origen actually held. This was done both by those who later condemned Origen, and by the Arians who appealed to him as their patron. However, it does not seem that he himself drew this conclusion, or even that he could have done so when his teaching as a whole is taken into account (Lonergan 1964a, 60–62; 1976a, 64–67).

divinity of the Son in saying that while the Father is eternal the Son is temporal. One also denies it if one maintains that the Son, but not the Father, was brought into being for the purpose of the creation and government of the world. Irenaeus had not broken free from the earlier uncritical viewpoint, but avoided falling into error on the matter by the simple expedient of ruling out all speculation into the manner of the Son's generation.[62] Clement and Origen did speculate on the matter, and indeed progressed beyond uncritical realism; thus they rejected the conception of the Son's divinity as a sharing of the quasi-material stuff of which the Father consists. But, resorting as they did to Platonic ideas and conceptions, they did not reach as clear a position on the matter as was soon to become possible (Lonergan 1964a, 137, 140, 143, 147).

All these uncertainties and confusions were dispelled by Arius, in his own way. He maintained that whatever derives its being from another, in any way at all, is a creature. Thus, he said, if one is to speak strictly, and exclude all metaphor, only the Father is ungenerated, eternal, and lacking all beginning. The Son is none of these things, but is the highest of the creatures created by the Father's will. It followed also that the Father had not always been Father, but had become so only at the time when he brought the Son into existence. Thus it was not in a literal sense that the Son was called the Word or Wisdom of God, since he had been made *through* God's word and the wisdom which is and has always been within God.[63] At one stage of their deliberations, the bishops at the Council of Nicea wished to include in the decree the statement of Alexander bishop of Alexandria, that the Son was the exact and in no way discrepant image of the Father.[64] But since they considered that Arian subterfuges were not adequately ruled out by this formula, they finally set it down that the Son is consubstantial with the Father (Lonergan 1964a, 64–65, 149).[65]

The formulation of this doctrine was what finally excluded both subordinationism and essentially Stoic or Platonic conceptions of the relations between the divine Persons. The use of the term *homoousios* (the Greek equivalent of the Latin *consubstantialis*) by the Council of Nicea has often been said to represent an influx of Greek metaphysics into Christian doctrine. This claim, Lonergan argues, is a fundamental mistake. According to G. Prestige, the term *homoousios*, prior to its use as a technical term by Christian theologians, originally meant simply "of one stuff," where this phrase is to be understood in a generic sense (Prestige 1936, 197, 209). (Thus two desks made out of the same *kind of* wood, or two dresses made out of the same *kind of* material, would be "consubstantial" in this sense.) How was it that this term ever came to be used for theological or dogmatic purposes? In

---

[62] *Adv. Haer.*, II, 28, 6.

[63] Cf. the profession of faith cited in Athanasius, *De Synodis*, 16; MG 26, 707–9.

[64] Alex. ep. Alex., *ad Alex ep. Thess.*, 12; MG 18, 566 BC.

[65] Athanasius, *De decr. nic. syn.*, 20; MG 25, 449C.

Scripture, the Son is referred to in such terms as "the image of God," and "the wisdom of God," and "the effulgence of God's splendor and the stamp of God's very being."[66] Since he is called the wisdom of God, it was only to be expected that the early Christian writers would understand as applying to him such passages as the following concerning the divine wisdom: "Like a fine mist she rises from the power of God, a pure effluence from the glory of the Almighty . . . She is the brightness that streams from everlasting light, the flawless mirror of the active power of God and the image of his goodness."[67] To these images the Fathers added others, such as those already mentioned—that the Son proceeded from the Father as child from parent, river from source, rays from the sun, light from light, and fire from fire. However, what is immediately at issue is not these images themselves, but the concept of "consubstantiality" which is to be grasped by insight into them (cf. Lonergan 1957, chap. 1).

As Athanasius himself says, the term "consubstantial" compendiously expresses that relationship of the Son to the Father which is conveyed in all these various expressions used in Scripture.[68] According to him, many examples of consubstantiality are to be found among corporeal creatures, and one should attend to the limitations of these when applying the term to God. Thus children are consubstantial with their parents, and yet may be sundered from them. But the divine Word can never be separated from his Father, nor the Father from his Word. Thus this aspect of their union may better be conveyed by the image of light and its shining.[69] The Son is indeed so closely and intimately present to the Father that he is his illuminative and creative power, without which he neither knows nor creates.[70] While the Son is other than the Father in that he is begotten as opposed to begetting, he is the same in that he is God.[71] Athanasius' thinking on the subject culminates in his rule. This is to the effect that what is true of the Father is true of the Son, except that the Son is not the Father[72]—which is what it is for the Son to be consubstantial with the Father. He illustrated and confirmed his point by citing a number of Scriptural terms and titles, e.g., "God," "Almighty," "Lord," "Light," "who takes away sins," which were applied to the Son as well as to the Father.[73] He concluded that the principle had general application because the Son had said that all that the Father has belongs to him, and

---

[66] 1 Cor. 1:24; Heb. 1:3.

[67] Wis. 7:25–26.

[68] Athanasius, *De synodis*, 41; MG 26, 765C. *Ad Afros*, 6; MG 26, 1040 AB.

[69] *De decretis nic. syn.*, 20; MG 25, 452C.

[70] *De synodis*, 52; MG 26, 785C-788B.

[71] *Orat. III contr. Arianos*, 4; MG 26, 328C-329B.

[72] *Ta auta legetai peri tou huiou, hosa legetai kai peri tou patros, chōris tou legesthai patēr.* MG 26, 329A. Cf. Lonergan 1972, 307.

[73] MG 26, 329B.

all that he has belongs to the Father (Lonergan 1964a, 83–86, 77; 1976a, sec. IX).

Athanasius distinguished between "creating" as God's production of creatures and "making" as creatures' production of one another. He derived this distinction from the fact that God is uniquely "he who is," while creatures have their existence entirely from God.[74] He articulated precisely the distinction between "unbegotten" and "uncreated"[75] in such a way as to show that if the Son *was* properly speaking the Son, he could not be a creature, whereas if he were a creature, he could not be the Son.[76] The Son is not brought into being out of nothing; therefore, he is not a creature. But it does not follow that he is from no principle whatever, since he is from the Father. Both the Son and creatures are from God, but whereas creatures are freely chosen and made by him, the Son arises from him as it were naturally.[77] Whatever is not a creature, is God; therefore the Son is God. And since there is only one God, the Son is the same God as the Father, and thus consubstantial with him (Lonergan 1964a, 61, 151).[78]

Lonergan compares the rule formulated by Athanasius, which gives the meaning of the term "consubstantial," to the electromagnetic equations formulated by Maxwell. While it conveys insights into what is sensible or imaginable, there is nothing sensible or imaginable which directly corresponds to it. Rather, it relates directly to concepts and judgments. It does not tell you anything of a direct or first-order kind about the Father or the Son. All that it tells you is that *if* anything is true of the Father, then by virtue of the fact that the Father is God, it is *also* true of the Son. What was taken over from Greek philosophy was not a *concept* or set of concepts, but rather a *technique*—the technique of formulating propositions about propositions about things, as opposed to directly about things. "Consubstantial" and its Greek equivalent were never philosophical terms. They were words which were in use in ordinary language, and were employed by the Fathers in a transferred or metaphorical sense for the special purpose of articulating and clarifying Christian belief in the face of the doctrines professed by the heretics (Lonergan 1964a, 86; 1976a, 99–101. Cf. 1974, 23).

The rule laid down by Athanasius, and the definition of consubstantiality implicit in it, has of course proved of the utmost importance for subsequent theology. It was the first step from the symbolic language and culturally-determined viewpoint of Scripture to the theoretical language and universal viewpoint of Catholic dogma.[79] Lonergan warns, however, that since this was

---

[74] *De decretis nic. syn.*, 11.

[75] *De synodis*, 46.

[76] *De decretis nic. syn.*, 13.

[77] *De syn.*, 40; MG 26, 764. *De syn.*, 35; MG 26, 754C; Ibid., 754D–E.

[78] *De syn.*, 48; MG 26, 778C.

[79] On the "universal viewpoint," see 10–11 above. Also Lonergan 1957, xxiv, 564–68, 738–39; 1972, 153.

only the first step towards the systematic articulation of Christian belief, the rule functions quite differently in the works of Athanasius and his contemporaries, on the one hand, and in those of much later Christian writers, on the other. In a fully systematic theology, such as was achieved by the great Scholastics, the consubstantiality of the Son with the Father is asserted within a broad technical and metaphysical framework.[80] Such a viewpoint should not be anachronistically attributed to Athanasius himself. Indeed, he did not even make use of the distinction between substance (*ousia*) and person (*hypostasis*), since for him both terms meant the same (Lonergan 1964a, 86–87).[81]

It is often maintained that Scripture remains within the categories of religious experience, while the Greek councils from Nicea onwards moved away from these categories to embrace Greek metaphysics. Lonergan admits that there is a fundamental change in viewpoint and in the manner in which belief is expressed between Scripture and the Greek councils. Nonetheless he insists that it is highly misleading to express the matter in the way just mentioned. As he sees it, implicit in acceptance of divine revelation in Scripture is what might be termed "dogmatic realism." That is to say, believers, however naive or sophisticated they may be, have almost always accepted that things are thus and thus, as God has revealed them to be, and not otherwise.

Of course it would be absurd to hold that the dogmatic realism involved in acceptance of the Word of God is always or usually explicit, that is, that Isaiah, Paul, or Athanasius were conscious of being dogmatic realists. But they did submit to the word of God, and they did act, speak, and write in accordance with what they believed to be so in the light of it. Lonergan remarks severely that to say that the biblical writers were concerned only with religious experience may conform very well with the interests and habits of mind of those inured to ways of thinking fashionable in our own century. But it cannot be admitted either by Catholics who believe in truths communicated by the word of God, or by historians who conceive their craft as an attempt to find out what people of the past actually did, said and thought, rather than as an instrument for polemics or apologetics. The fact is that Isaiah and Paul did not regard themselves as expressing their religious experience, but as proclaiming what they believed to be so in accordance with the word of God. Religious experience as such is nothing but a state of the subject who undergoes it. Yet this by no means applies, or was taken by these authors as applying, to what is conveyed by the word of God (Lonergan 1964a, 106–7). (It is perhaps worth noting that Lonergan's argument at this point is not directed against the non-Christian and non-Catholic view that the prophets and apostles *thought* that they were communicating truths

[80] Cf. pp. 91–2 below.
[81] Athanasius, *Epist. ad Afros*, 4; MG 26, 1036B.

about God, but *in fact* were simply evincing their religious experience. What he is attacking is the notion that they were not really concerned with stating what they believed to be the case, but only with expressing their inner experience.)

The Council of Nicea, in using the term "consubstantial" as it did, does no more than make explicit the dogmatic realism already implicit in Scripture. As has already been said, all that the consubstantiality of the Father and the Son amounts to is that everything which is truly spoken of the Father is truly spoken of the Son. Given dogmatic realism, what is truly spoken is what corresponds to a real state of affairs. Thus the hypothesis of an influx of Greek metaphysics into Christianity from Nicea onwards is quite superfluous. It seems the more so, the more one considers the nature of contemporary Greek metaphysical systems, and their actual influence on Christian thinking.[82] Of course, to say all this is not to imply that the dogmatic realism implicit in Scripture became explicit without any assistance from Greek culture. It is one thing to assign the source of dogmatic realism, another to describe adequately the process by which what was implicit became explicit. Unless there had been Gnostics, Marcionites, Sabellians, and Arians, and unless there had been bishops who felt it incumbent on them to answer heretics not just with excommunication but with a more exact profession of faith, the advance in doctrine which has been described would never have taken place (Lonergan 1964a, 108).

It may be asked what is the bearing of dogmatic realism, and of the slow emergence of its implications over the history of the development of Christian doctrine, on the distinction between naive and critical realism which is basic to Lonergan's thought.[83] Now everyone acknowledges that there is a difference between real and unreal; but people differ when it comes to assigning the criteria of reality. Uncritical realists will say that, for instance, a particular mountain is real, in that they are able to see it with their eyes, walk on it with their feet, and feel it with their hands. Since the matter is so clear and obvious to them, they are apt to resent any other criterion which may be suggested to them as due to sheer stupidity or perversity. (The criteria which they take for granted prove troublesome, of course, when the reality of other minds, of the theoretical entities postulated in science, and of the things and events of the past are in question, for none of these can be directly seen or heard or felt.) Critical realists concede that the mountain is visible to the eyes, firm beneath the feet, and palpable to the hands. But they insist that its reality consists in the fact that its existence is to be affirmed in a true judgment, stated on sufficient evidence. (On this criterion, the troublesome cases present no difficulty.) Dogmatic realists, just by accepting as true what has been revealed by God, which goes beyond what is

---

[82] See pp. 65–70 above.
[83] For an useful account of this distinction, see Tyrrell 1974, 20–22.

available to sense-experience, agree in principle with the critical realist, though *why* they should do so they are unable clearly to say. Thus they are apt to adulterate their dogmatic realism with elements derived from uncritical realism.[84]

It is a simple matter to see that this kind of thing is going on in the writings of the ante-Nicene Christian Fathers. Men and women who assented to the revealed Word of God in such a way that they spread their faith over the whole Roman empire, and gave their lives for it in martyrdom, were certainly dogmatic realists. But merely dogmatic realists do not really know the full reasons for their position, and likewise fail to grasp all the consequences which flow from it. They keep slipping back into assumptions deriving from uncritical realism. They maintain in effect that the real is what is to be known through true judgment, yet they are apt also to assume that it must take up a certain amount of room in space. They do not really doubt that for two things to be distinct is for one of them not to be the other, but they may say at the same time that things can be distinct only so far as they occupy different segments of space or time. It is evident to them that effects depend on their causes, but they are inclined to envisage this dependence in terms of branches growing from trees, children sprung from their parents, rays emitted from the sun, one firebrand lit from another, and so on. These contradictions provide a basis upon which the dialectical process may operate. What is required in addition is simply the light of reason, which leads either to heresy or advance in doctrine. And so, given the occasions provided by the heresies, the process of dialectic gradually expels uncritical realism, and makes dogmatic realism more conscious of itself and its implications (Lonergan 1964a, 108–9; 1976a, 127–37).

What, in brief, was achieved by the Council of Nicea, according to Lonergan's account? First, it represents the fruit of systematic reflection upon the teaching of Scripture, rather than mere reiteration of that teaching in its own terms. Scripture teaches many things about the Father, and many about the Son. When these are compared with each other, the conclusion is yielded that the same things are true of the Son as of the Father, except that the Son is not the Father. And this is as much as to say that the Son is consubstantial with the Father. Second, there is a transition from what is true about the Father and the Son in relation to us, and what is true of them in themselves. For Scripture speaks of what relates directly to us, of the Son who was sent among us by the Father, who has died and risen again for us, who now reigns over us in heaven, and who will come to judge us in the future. But in the process of reflecting on these statements, and in noting that whatever is true of the Father is also true of the Son, we leave ourselves out of account and compare the Father and the Son with one another as they are in themselves (Lonergan 1964a, 109).

---

[84] On the two sorts of realism, see pp. 1–10 above.

Once the question of the Son's divinity and consubstantiality with the Father had been settled, there inevitably arose the same question with regard to the Holy Spirit. In 362, the Synod of Alexandria condemned those who held that the Holy Spirit was a creature, and added that this was to maintain the Arian heresy, implicitly if not in so many words. The so-called "Macedonians,"[85] who became a sect only after about 380—before that they had been referred to just as "certain persons" or "Pneumatomachoi" (Spirit-bashers)—apparently held that the Holy Spirit was neither God, nor properly to be included among creatures (Lonergan 1964a, 157–58).

Here as elsewhere, Lonergan complains, the issue is confused by those ensnared in the opposite errors of archaism and anachronism. Archaists rightly point out that explicit references to the Holy Spirit in the early writers, as opposed to those to the Father and the Son, are comparatively few and late, and seem at first to signify rather a divine power or impersonal gift than a distinct person. Then they go on to ascribe a kind of binitarianism, or belief that there are two divine Persons, to the New Testament writers and their immediate successors. Anachronists, on the other hand, detect in these writers an elaborated theological system such as was only developed later, implying in effect that the First Vatican Council was wrong in claiming that knowledge and understanding by the Church of the revealed word of God increases with the passage of time (Lonergan 1964a, 158).[86]

The word "spirit" (*pneuma*) is used in many senses in the New Testament. It is applied to the "unclean spirits." It is used in reference to the principle of life, where it is said that a body without a spirit is dead,[87] and that a human person gives up his spirit as he dies.[88] The term is also used of the principle of knowledge, emotion and morality in human beings.[89] However, the word is employed in a special manner quite distinct from all of these. Christians speak of the Holy Spirit, or the Spirit of God, or the Spirit of Christ, in a special sense at once peculiar to themselves and well-known among them. For example, we hear of those Ephesians who did not know that there was a Holy Spirit,[90] and of the revelation made through the Spirit of God which seems foolishness to carnal men.[91] Again, the criterion of possession of the Spirit is what a person says about Jesus,[92] and reference is made to the Spirit of Truth which the world cannot accept, but which dwells with Christians and is in them.[93]

---

[85] Macedonius, bishop of Constantinople from 342 to 369, does not seem to have been regarded as a heresiarch until after his death.

[86] Denzinger 1963 (DS in subsequent references), 3020.

[87] Jas. 2:26.

[88] Matt. 27:50; Luke 23:46; John 19:30; Acts 7:59.

[89] Mark 2:8; Matt. 5:3; Acts 17:16.

[90] Acts 19:2–7.

[91] 1 Cor. 2:10–16.

[92] 1 Cor. 12:3; cf. John 15:26.

[93] John 14:16–17; cf. 14:25–26, 16:7–15. Also 1 Cor. 6:19; 1 Thess. 6:8.

The Holy Spirit is said to have spoken through prophets and inspired men of old,[94] for example through David and Isaiah[95] and in more recent times through Elizabeth, Zachariah, Simeon, and John the Baptist.[96] She is present at the conception of Jesus and at his baptism.[97] Jesus is full of the Holy Spirit, is anointed with the Holy Spirit, and works by the Spirit of God.[98] The Spirit of the Father speaks in the apostles, to whom she is promised and given at the Last Supper, and after the Resurrection.[99] She is given also to their successors, to Paul and Barnabas, to the baptised, and ultimately to the Gentiles.[100] The Spirit rules the Church, for example the community at Antioch.[101] She directs the apostles and other leaders, for example Peter, Philip the deacon, the leaders of the Ephesian community, and the council at Jerusalem.[102] She is so intimately involved in the mission of the apostles, that to resist them is to resist the Holy Spirit, and to lie to Peter is to lie to the Holy Spirit and to God.[103] She is a witness together with the apostles, and is the source of their consolation and joy (Lonergan 1964a, 160).[104]

One may conclude from all of this that the New Testament writers suppose the Holy Spirit to be a real being, distinct from all created things, and divine. Lonergan notes that this is a *conclusion* from what is said in the New Testament, which of course includes no direct statement to this effect. But all the same, he insists, the conclusion is well founded. It is the most serious of all blasphemies to attribute the work of the Holy Spirit to demons;[105] this could hardly be the case if she were a mere creature. Human beings receive from the Holy Spirit what they receive from God, remission of sins, and rebirth into new life.[106] However, while the Spirit is assumed to be divine, she is assumed equally to be distinct from Father and Son. This may be gathered from the order of salvation, in which the ascension of the Son is followed by the outpouring of the Spirit.[107] It may also be inferred from the threefold name in which Christians are baptised,[108] and from the exemplar of Christian baptism, in which the Spirit descends upon the Son from the

---

[94] 2 Pet. 1:21.
[95] Mark 12:36; Acts 28:25.
[96] Luke 1:15, 41, 67; 2:25–27.
[97] Matt. 1:18, 20; Luke 1:35. Matt. 3:16; Mark 1:10; Luke 3:21–2.
[98] Luke 4:1, 14, 18; Acts 10:38; Mark 3:21–30.
[99] Matt. 10:19–20; John 14:16–17, 26; John 20:22.
[100] Acts 9:17, 11:24; 2:38, 8:17, 19:6; 10:44–47.
[101] Acts 8:2, 4.
[102] Acts 4:8; 10:19; 11:12; 8:29; 39; 20:28; 15:28.
[103] Acts 7:51; 5:3–4.
[104] Acts 5:32; 9:31, 13:52.
[105] Mark 3:21–30; Matt. 12:24–32.
[106] 2 Pet. 1:21; 1 Cor. 2:10, 12; John 20:22–23 (cf. Mark 2:5–7); 1 Cor. 6:11, John 3:5, Tit. 3:5.
[107] Acts 2:33, Gal. 4:4–6, John 14:16–17, 26, 15:26.
[108] Matt. 28:19.

Father.[109] It may be inferred also from Paul's enumerations of the divine Persons.[110] Clearest of all on this matter is John's Gospel, which tells of the Son speaking to the apostles both of the Father and of the coming Paraclete. This is the Spirit of Truth whom the Father will bestow at the Son's request, who will be sent by the Son from the Father and will bear witness to the Son, and who will speak not from herself but what she receives from the Son and the Father (Lonergan 1964a, 160–62).[111]

Clement of Rome writes that Christians have one God, one Christ, and one Spirit of grace poured out upon them.[112] Justin names all three Persons when he describes baptism[113] and the eucharist.[114] In refuting the charge that Christians are atheists, he states that they adore the Father, the Son, the host of angels, and the Holy Spirit.[115] In connection with the same accusation of atheism, Athenagoras says that Christians proclaim God the Father, God the Son, and the Holy Spirit, united in power yet distinct in order, and that they acknowledge in addition a multitude of angels and ministers.[116] Theophilus of Antioch states that the first three days of creation described in the Book of Genesis, which preceded the creation of the luminaries, are an image of the Trinity, that is to say, of God, God's Word, and God's Wisdom.[117] Irenaeus similarly refers to the Son and the Spirit as God's Word and Wisdom, adding that all the angels serve and are subject to them.[118]

Tertullian speaks readily of "the three" and "the Trinity," and says explicitly that the three are of one substance.[119] Hippolytus, on the other hand, does not appear to hold that the Spirit is a Person in the way that the Father and the Son are, though he does plainly assert that there are three in God.[120] Clement of Alexandria actually claims the doctrine of the Trinity is to be found not only in Scripture, but in the works of Plato as well.[121] Origen says that the Son was known by some who were not Christians, but that the Holy Spirit was known only to those who learned from the law and prophets and acknowledged Christ as their Lord.[122] He regards belief in the Trinity as part of the rule of faith,[123] and explicitly distinguishes Father and Son as

---

[109] Mark 1:10.

[110] Gal. 4:4–6; 1 Cor. 12:4–6; 2 Cor. 13:14; Rom. 15:16; Eph. 2:18; 4:3–6. Cf. Tit. 3:4–7.

[111] John 14:16–17, 15:26, 16:13–15.

[112] *The First Epistle to the Corinthians*, 46, 6 (Rouet de Journel 1962 [EP in subsequent references], 23).

[113] I *Apol.*, 61; EP 126.

[114] Ibid., 65; EP 128.

[115] Ibid., 13; EP 113.

[116] Athenagoras, *Legatio*, 10; EP 164.

[117] *Ad Autol.*, 2, 15; EP 180.

[118] *Adv. Haer.*, IV, 7, 4.

[119] *Adv. Prax.*, 2.

[120] Hippolytus, *C. haer. Noeti*, 14; MG 10, 822 BC, A.

[121] *Strom.*, V, 14; 103, 1.

[122] *De Princ.*, I, 3, 1.

[123] *De Princ.*, Praef., 4.

"hypostases" or Persons.[124] However, since his reflections on the relations between the Father and the Son are, from the point of view of later developments at least, rather less happy, it is hardly surprising that the same applies to his account of the Holy Spirit. In expounding the statement of Scripture that all things were made through the Word,[125] he says that the Holy Spirit is superior in dignity to all *else* that was made through the Word (Lonergan 1964a, 171, 174).[126]

The post-Nicene Fathers clearly state the Holy Spirit's divinity, as well as her distinctness from the other Persons. Thus Athanasius says that all that the Son has from the Father is also in the Spirit through the Son. As the Son is God in virtue of the fact that all that is true of the Father is true also of him, so the Holy Spirit is God, and thus consubstantial with the Father and the Son, for the same reason.[127] Basil argues that if the Holy Spirit were a creature, she would be holy only contingently and not necessarily, and thus capable of evil. In that case she would not be what in fact she is, the very fount of holiness. It follows that the Holy Spirit is not a creature, and whatever is not a creature is consubstantial with God.[128] Whereas Athanasius emphasises the consubstantiality of the Persons, Basil lays stress on their community of operation. The Father, Son, and Holy Spirit, he says, together vivify, sanctify, illumine, and console.[129] Both of them teach that the Spirit is essentially holy, and that creatures have what holiness they may have by participation.[130] Gregory of Nazianzus says that just as the Son is not the Father, but what the Father is, so, likewise, the Spirit is not the Son, but what the Son is. Therefore the Spirit is God, and consubstantial with Father and Son.[131] He speaks of a special kind and degree of holiness in the Holy Spirit, as distinct from creatures, as though this were a fact generally acknowledged (Lonergan 1964a, 175–77).[132]

[124] *In Ioan.*, II, 10.

[125] John 1:2–3.

[126] *In Ioan.*, II, 10.

[127] Athanasius, *Ad Serap.*, III, 1; MG 26, 625; EP 783.

[128] Basil, Epist., 8, 10; MG 32, 261; EP 783.

[129] Epist., 189, 7; MG 32, 693; EP 920.

[130] Athanasius, *Ad Serap.*, I, 24; MG 26, 585; EP 780. *Adv. Eunom.*, III, 2; MG 29, 660; EP 941.

[131] Gregory of Nazianzus, *Orat.*, 31 (theol. 5), 9 and 10; MG 36, 144A; EP 996.

[132] *Orat.*, 25, 16; MG 35, 1221; EP 983.

# Chapter 6

## SUBSTANCE AND PERSONS

If the fundamental advance in doctrine made at the Council of Nicea came about as a result of controversy with the Arians, its consolidation was due to disputes with the Eunomians. Eunomius and his followers maintained that it was of the essence of the divine to be in no way derivative. On this basis, they were able to construct many arguments against the doctrine of the Trinity. It was as a result of their activities that the Fathers, especially Basil, Gregory of Nazianzus, and Gregory of Nyssa, were virtually compelled to evolve the doctrine further and to elaborate it systematically (Lonergan 1964a, 183).

Lonergan points out that the terms "substance" and "person" (*ousia* and *hupostasis*) only gradually came to be used to articulate the unity and distinctions within God. Athanasius, among many others, used the terms in exactly the same sense.[1] The Stoics, however, did use the terms to mark a distinction which to some extent anticipates the one made by later Christian theologians. By *ousia* they meant the material principle by virtue of which anything was real, and by *hupostasis*, that on account of which any real thing differed from any other thing.[2] Now Origen clearly taught that there were three in God, and said that the Father and the Son were each a *hupostasis* (Lonergan 1976a, 56).[3] And although Athanasius himself did not use the terminological distinction, he certainly grasped very clearly what was at issue in its use. In one famous dispute, Athanasius asked the party who affirmed that there were three *hupostases* whether they meant this in a tritheist or Arian sense. Did they mean that the three in God are three separate individuals like three men or of three different kinds like gold, silver, and bronze? They replied that such was very far from their intention. He then asked the opposed party, who maintained that there was only one *hupostasis*, whether they meant this in the Sabellian sense of there being no real distinction in God. They in turn promptly denied this, protesting that they were concerned only to deny that divinity, or nature, or *ousia* were distinct in Father, Son, and Holy Spirit. By then it was clear that the dispute was

---

[1] *Epist. ad Afros*, 4; MG 26, 1036B; Jerome, *Epist.*, 15, 4; Migne 1844–64 (ML in subsequent references) 22, 357.

[2] On Stoic influences on doctrinal development, see Lonergan 1976a, 39, 66–67, 105, 115, 117, etc.

[3] Lonergan 1976a, 56. *Contra Celsum*, VIII, 12; MG 11, 1333.

merely verbal.[4] But whatever Athanasius' practice on the matter, there is no doubt, as Lonergan says, that the formula that in God there is one *ousia* (substance) and three *hupostases* (persons) does effectively and concisely exclude Sabellianism (which identifies the persons), tritheism (which multiplies the substance), and Arianism (which denies the consubstantiality of the Persons). The necessity of such a formula may be gauged from the experience of the unfortunate Basil, who was accused of tritheism when he combatted Sabellianism, and of Sabellianism when he argued against tritheism. He ruefully compared himself to the lamb who won an argument with the wolf, but for all that was unable to save his skin (Lonergan 1964a, 191–93).[5]

The theologians of the time were much exercised, as well they might be, with the question of how oneness and multiplicity could be reconciled in God. Athanasius said that the Father and Son should be compared to the sun and its shining rather than to two suns.[6] Basil explained that the Son was in the Father, and the Father in the Son, and that what the one was, the other was also. The Son is called the "image" of the Father in Scripture,[7] and where there is a king together with the image of that king, it is wrong to say that there are two kings. The power of Father and Son is not sundered, nor is their glory divided.[8] Gregory of Nyssa pointed out that Christians differed from Jews by believing in the Word and the Spirit as well as in the Father, from the Greeks in believing in but one God. What remains from the Jewish conception is unity of substance, and what remains from the Greek is distinction of Persons.[9] From Tertullian onwards, the Latin Fathers distinguished between person and substance. But a misapprehension on their part that "hupostasis" was the equivalent of "substantia," rather than of "persona," caused a good deal of trouble. Jerome, when he visited the East, was expected to subscribe to the formula that there are three *hupostases* in God, and took violent exception. He wrote a very angry letter on the subject to Pope Damasus, going on as though acknowledging three *hupostases* were tantamount to admitting three substances.[10] It may have been for this reason that the orthodoxy of Basil, and that of other Eastern theologians who acknowledged three "hupostases," was not recognised for a time in the West (Lonergan 1964a, 187–88, 195).

In what respect are the Persons really distinct? According to Athanasius' rule, the same things are true of the Son as are true of the Father, except that only the Father is Father. For the Father to be thus distinct, there must be

---

[4] Athanasius, *Tomus ad Antiochenos*, 5 and 6; MG 42, 432–33. Cf. Lonergan 1974, 25–26.

[5] Basil, *Epist.*, 189, 2; MG 32, 686B.

[6] *Orat.* 3 *c. Arian.*, 15; MG 26, 352C.

[7] E.g., Col. 1:15.

[8] *De Spiritu S.*, 45; MG 32, 149BC.

[9] *Orat. catech.*, 3; MG 45, 18.

[10] Cf. Tertullian, *Adv. Prax.*, 2; Novatian, *De Trin.*, 31; Hippolytus, *C. haer. Noet.*, 14. Jerome, *Epist.*, 15; ML 22, 356–57.

some real characteristic in him by virtue of which he is not the Son, and vice-versa; and the same applies to the Holy Spirit in relation to the other Persons. As has already been said, it was the Arians and the Eunomians who provided the Church with the occasion to come to a clear mind on the matter. By making the concepts "unbegotten" and "uncreated" identical in meaning, they could argue that only the Father is really God. The so-called "Athanasian Creed" opposed them by laying it down "that the Father is neither made nor created nor begotten; that the Son is from the Father alone, not made nor created but begotten; that the Holy Spirit is from the Father and the Son, neither made nor created nor begotten but proceeding."[11] Lonergan suggests that a clue to the properties which distinguish each individual Person is to be found in the Gospel of John, in which the epithet "only-begotten" is applied to the Son.[12] If the Son is really the only-begotten, then there can be no other who is begotten. At the very beginning of the Arian controversy, Alexander bishop of Alexandria said that the Son was a perfect being, just as the Father was, differing from him only in being begotten, and added that the begetting of the Son was not temporal.[13] Basil answered the Eunomians with the statement that the term "unbegotten" was to be understood not of the divine essence or substance, but as the distinguishing property of a Person.[14] "Begotten" and "unbegotten," he explained, are characteristics or properties which, while they are *in* one substance, do not signify the substance as such or what pertains to it (Lonergan 1964a, 195–97).[15]

Gregory of Nazianzus applied the theory of distinct personal properties to the Holy Spirit. He said that it is common to the Persons to be divine, and that it follows from this that they are uncreated. It is common to the Son and the Holy Spirit that they are from the Father. It is peculiar to the Father that he begets, to the Son that he is begotten, and to the Holy Spirit that she proceeds; unbegottenness *(agennesia)* is thus characteristic of the Father, begottenness *(gennesis)* of the Son, and sent-out-ness *(ekpempsis)* of the Holy Spirit.[16] In attributing such a property to the Holy Spirit, Gregory was able to counter the gibe made by the Macedonians—that the Holy Spirit was either begotten or unbegotten, and that if she were unbegotten, there would be two which were unbegotten, but that if she were begotten, she would have to be either the Son's sibling or the Father's grandchild.[17] The Holy Spirit who proceeds from the Father,[18] since she proceeds from him, is not a

[11] DS 75–76.
[12] John 1:14, 18; 3:16, 18.
[13] Alex. ep. Alex. *ad Alex. ep. Thess.*, XII; MG 18, 566C, 567B.
[14] *Adversus Eunomium*, I, 19; MG 29, 556AB.
[15] Ibid., II, 28; MG 29, 637 AB.
[16] *Orat.* 25, 16; MG 35, 1221.
[17] *Orat.* 31, 7; MG 36, 140C.
[18] John 15:26.

creature; since she is unbegotten, is not the Son; and since she mediates between Father and Son, is none other than God.[19] In this passage, the term Gregory used for the distinctive property of the Holy Spirit is "proceedingness" *(ekporeusis)* (Lonergan 1964a, 197).

That the properties peculiar to each Person might be a matter of their relations each to the others had already been guessed before the Arian controversy. Thus Dionysius of Alexandria, in the course of defending his own orthodoxy, said that in referring to the Father one indirectly refers to the Son of whom he is Father, and vice-versa.[20] Already in the earlier stages of the Arian controversy, there were some who suggested that the Persons were distinct only in virtue of their mutual relations. This may be inferred from Arius' own *rejection* of such an account in his letter to Alexander bishop of Alexandria.[21] Both Athanasius and Hilary called attention to the fact that the relations of Fatherhood and Sonship implied one another. Athanasius said that whoever speaks of the Father implies that the Son exists also,[22] and Hilary, that to confess the Father is also to confess the Son, since only through the Son is the Father the Father.[23]

Gregory of Nazianzus mentioned the following Eunomian objection. The Father is Father by virtue either of his essence or his operation. If he is Father in virtue of his essence, then the Son, since he is not the Father, does not have the divine essence. But if he is Father in virtue of his action or operation, then the Son is made by him and thus a creature.[24] Gregory responded to the dilemma by claiming that Fatherhood is a matter neither of essence nor of operation, but of relation, between the Father and the Son.[25] Basil wrote to similar effect, but explained the matter more fully. He made a distinction between terms like "man," "horse" and "ox," which designate a thing as it is in itself, and terms like "son," "servant" and "friend," which designate a thing in relation to some other thing. He said that the terms designating the Persons of the Trinity are of the latter type (Lonergan 1964a, 198–200).[26] An obvious objection to this is that the term "Holy Spirit," unlike the terms "Father" and "Son," does not of itself signify anything in terms of a relation. Indeed, since the term is understood in a non-relative way, when applied to God it must signify the divine substance, since God is both holy and a spirit. Augustine noted the difficulty, and after searching the Scriptures he discovered that the Holy Spirit is called the "gift of God."[27] Evidently a gift as such is related both to a giver and a receiver. Further texts

---

[19] *Orat.* 31, 8; MG 36, 141B.

[20] Cf. Athanasius, *De sent. Dionys.*, 17; MG 25, 504C–D.

[21] Opitz 1934, III, 13, 11–12.

[22] *Orat.* 3 c. Ar., 6; MG 26, 333A. *De decr. nic. syn.*, 30; MG 25, 473A.

[23] Hilary, *De Trin.*, vii, 31; ML 10, 226B.

[24] *Orat.*, 29, 16; MG 36, 93C.

[25] Ibid., col. 96A. Cf. *Orat.*, 23, 7 and 11; MG 35, 1160C and 1161C.

[26] Basil, *Adv. Eunom.*, II, 9; MG 29, 588B–590.

[27] Acts 8:20.

established that the Holy Spirit was the gift both of the Father and of the Son (Lonergan 1964a, 200, 221).[28]

The Council of Florence, following the lead of Anselm,[29] stated that all is one in God except where a mutual opposition of relations is involved.[30] This, as Lonergan remarks, amounts to a summary answer to the question of how it can be that although there are three distinct Persons who are God, there are not three Gods. Gregory of Nazianzus maintained that the properties "not being begotten," "being begotten," and "proceeding," distinguish one as Father, one as Son, and one as Holy Spirit, without the unity of the divine nature being impugned (Lonergan 1964a, 224–27).[31] The matter was still more clearly apprehended by Gregory of Nyssa, who maintained that the three are distinct from one another neither spatially, nor temporally, nor in will, counsel, and operation.[32] The Son has everything that the Father has, and is everything that the Father is, except that he is not the Father, and the same applies to the Holy Spirit in relation to the Son.[33] Gregory also made a series of distinctions which laid the foundation for all subsequent speculation on the subject, between *what* something is and *how* it is, between principle and derivative, and between immediately and mediately derivative.[34] In God *what* is is the divine essence. *How* it is is a matter of the properties and modes of existence which distinguish the Persons, and of their relations each to the others. The "principle" is the Father, the "immediately derivative" the Son, and the "mediately derivative" the Holy Spirit (Lonergan 1964a, 203–4).[35]

Lonergan notes that the exigences of Christian doctrine impelled thinkers to make certain purely philosophical distinctions which they would perhaps not otherwise have made.[36] Among these was a modification of the doctrine, derived from Aristotle, that number presupposes matter and quantity.[37] Aristotle's point is that in the normal case at least where there are two or more individuals of exactly the same type, the matter of which each consists must be different from that of which the others consist, or there will be no grounds for any distinction. But if Aristotle were right on this matter, it would follow either that God was material or that there were not three Persons in God. The medieval Scholastic philosophers sought to resolve the difficulty by distinguishing between predicamental and transcendental number, the former of which presupposed matter and quantity, while the

---

[28] *De Trin.*, V, xi, 12; ML 42, 919. John 15:26; Rom. 8:9.

[29] *De processione Spiritus sancti*, 2. ML 158, 288.

[30] DS 1330.

[31] Orat., 31, 9; MG 36, 141C.

[32] *Ad Graecos ex communibus nationibus;* MG 45, 180C.

[33] *Contra Eunom.*, II; MG 45, 493B.

[34] In Greek: *ti esti, pōs esti, aitios, to prosechōs ek tou prōtou, to dia tou prosechōs ek tou prōtou.*

[35] *Ad Ablabium quod non sunt tres dei*, MG 45, 134A–D.

[36] See especially "The Origins of Christian Realism" (Lonergan 1974, 239–61).

[37] Aristotle, *Metaphysics*, XII, 8, 1074a33; XIV, 2, 1089b34.

latter was known through affirmations and negations.[38] It is easy to see that the Scholastic position is fully vindicated by Lonergan's theory of knowledge, according to which what is real, including the real distinction between one thing and another, is to be known by judgments affirmed with sufficient reason. Material difference is in that case not necessarily the only possible difference between two entities of exactly the same type.[39] In the case of the Trinity, Scripture and the tradition of the Church provide grounds for affirming that there is in God one who "begets," one who "is begotten," and one who "proceeds." To beget is distinct from being begotten, to proceed is distinct from giving rise to the proceeding. (How "begetting" and "proceeding" are to be more exactly conceived, on Lonergan's account, will appear when the psychological analogy is discussed.)[40] Thus we have a set of distinctions known by affirmation and negation based upon sufficient reason, which do not involve matter and quantity. The Scholastics maintained that number in God was transcendental, both in the case of the divine essence, which is numerically one, and in that of the divine Persons, who are numerically three (Lonergan 1964a, 205–6).

But the fourth century Fathers had not discovered this technical solution to the problem, and they coped with it in a more informal way. Thus, as Lonergan reminds us, they are easily misunderstood by those who are prone to the anachronist blunder of foisting on earlier authors conceptions and distinctions only arrived at at a later time. For example, when Evagrius of Pontus says, "We confess God as one not in number but in nature,"[41] the unwary may take him to imply that God is not numerically one, but one only in species or type as "man" is. This, of course, would mean that he was a polytheist. However, what he really held on the matter is clear from what immediately follows: "Whatever can be said to be one in number, is not really one or simple in nature; but we all confess God as simple and incomposite."[42] Although these earlier authors did not have the precise terminological means of expression available to later writers, one should not be misled into thinking that the technical terms, once evolved, do other than convey briefly and accurately what previously had been expressed in a more informal and roundabout way (Lonergan 1964a, 210–13).[43]

[38] Cf. Thomas Aquinas, *Summa Theologica*, I, xxx, 3.

[39] On the grounds of difference according to a fully critical metaphysics, cf. Lonergan 1957, chap. 16.

[40] See pp. 85–90 below.

[41] Quoted by Basil, *Epist.*, 8, 2; MG 32, 248.

[42] Cf. also Gregory of Nyssa, *C. Eunom.*, I; MG 45, 312B. *Quod non sunt tres dii;* MG 45, 131A. Basil, *De Spiritu S.*, 18, 44; MG 32, 149A.

[43] On the meaning of the technical terms coined by the Greek Councils, in the context of those councils themselves, the following is worth quoting: "What is a person or hypostasis? It is in the Trinity what there are three of and in the Incarnation what there is one of. What is a nature? In the Trinity it is what there is one of and in the Incarnation it is what there are two of" (Lonergan 1974, 259).

# Chapter 7

# SYSTEMATICS OF THE TRINITY

Lonergan says that if we are to do for our own age what the great Scholastics did for theirs, we must apprehend the Christian faith not only in terms of metaphysics, as they did, but in terms of the interiority in which a truly critical metaphysics must be grounded (Lonergan 1972, 343). He himself tries to show how, by attending to our own operations as conscious subjects, we may achieve such understanding as is intrinsically possible for us in this life of the mystery of the Trinity. His object is not to *prove* the doctrine, which indeed he thinks is impossible. But that it cannot be proved does not imply that we can achieve no measure of *understanding* of it (Lonergan 1964b, 68).[1]

The aspects of our consciousness to which Lonergan proposes that we attend for this purpose are these. We know by experience the difference between simply repeating from memory something that we have learned and really *understanding* it in such a way that we can expound it in all sorts of different ways. Again, we know what it is to be subject to a kind of constraint to propound the *judgment* that something is the case or is not the case, when we realise that there is sufficient reason for us to do so. Finally, we are aware of the difference between the kind of *decision* which is as it ought to be and the kind which is irrational or immoral. Briefly, we all know what it is to be more or less intelligent, reasonable, and responsible. Let us call what is present when one comes to understand, judges with sufficient reason, or decides appropriately and honorably, an "intellectual emanation," since in each case some intellectual activity is involved or presupposed, which emanates from the conscious subject or person. When we think about these "intellectual emanations," it becomes clear that we have at least two types or levels of consciousness, according to whether they are present or not. In our merely sensitive consciousness, we more or less passively undergo sensations, images, desires, fears, pleasures, and so on. But our intellectual consciousness, which consists in these intellectual emanations, is more active than passive. It is at this intellectual level of consciousness that we

---

[1] The "Semirationalists" of the nineteenth century held that the divine mysteries were demonstrable, and accordingly tried to prove them; but their view was condemned by the First Vatican Council (DS 3041). Lonergan remarks that if the Semirationalists erred by excess, others have done so by deficiency, in denying that a human being in this life can achieve even an imperfect understanding of these matters.

inquire in order to understand, ponder evidence in order to judge, and judge how things are in order to decide and act appropriately. And it is this intellectual level of consiousness which provides the necessary basis for such understanding of the Trinity as we may achieve during this life (Lonergan 1964b, 70–72).[2]

If we should try to argue that we have no experience of the intellectual emanations which have just been described, our argument would be self-destructive, since the very process of arguing involves them. For, as Lonergan points out, either our judgment to that effect would be based on our grasp of sufficient reason, in which case we would *then* at least have the experience of judging on the basis of sufficient reason, even if we had never had it before; or it would not, in which case there would be no reason for anyone else to regard our "argument" as an argument at all, let alone to take it seriously. Again, our arguing about the matter will either be based on a sincere and honorable decision to try to get at the truth, or it will not. If it does not, it will again be pointless for anyone to take us seriously; if it does, we will once more by that very fact have had experience of what Lonergan calls an "intellectual emanation." It is important to emphasise that it is one thing to *have* the experiences in question, as every person does, but quite another to *draw attention to* and *objectify* them as has just been done (Lonergan 1964a, 278–9).[3] This last procedure is of the essence of what Lonergan calls the differentiation of consciousness of interiority.

Our autonomy as human beings, in accordance with which judgment proceeds from understanding, and moral choice from judgment, is exercised in three principal ways. First, we exercise it in practical affairs, when we decide what to do, on the basis of understanding and judgment, in the circumstances of ordinary life. Second, we exercise it in science and speculation, when we inquire into the nature of things, and come to judge how they are and how they have come to be so. Third, we exercise it existentially, when we wonder about ourselves, make judgments about how we should be and how we can make ourselves so, and choose accordingly so far as we are able. Lonergan suggests that the analogy of the Trinity which is to be found in human consciousness is based on this third form of expression of human autonomy. For when we inquire into the mystery of the Trinity, we are not studying God in God's creative or active capacity, which corresponds to our own practical autonomy. Nor are we studying God as knowing everything which is other than God, which corresponds to our science and speculation. But we are concerned with God in God's eternal conception and approbation of God, which is to apply to God the analogy of our existential autonomy (Lonergan 1964b, 90–91).

The gist of the matter is that, in order to account for the data of revelation

[2] On these basic mental acts, cf. chap. 1 above. Also Lonergan 1968, chaps. 1 and 2.
[3] Cf. pp. 1–8 above; and Lonergan 1957, chap. 11.

in Scripture and the tradition of the Church, Lonergan proposes that God, who is unrestricted understanding, forms a perfectly adequate conception or "inner word" of God. As the conception so formed and issuing from the understanding, God arises from God, Son is "begotten" by Father. The love which arises in accordance with the understanding and conception is also God arising from God, that is, the Holy Spirit "proceeding from" Father and Son together.[4] Now what emanates in such a way from God cannot be a creature, and consequently cannot be other than God. For a creature to come into existence is for God to bring into being something external to and other than God, but this emanation takes place within the divine consciousness itself. Furthermore, as eminently reasonable and responsible, it takes place by a kind of necessary exigence within the divine consciousness, but this is certainly not the case with the production of creatures, which God is absolutely free to create or not to create. What are at issue are those two kinds of intellectual emanation, by which a conscious being honorably loves because of true affirmation, and truly affirms because of understanding of adequate evidence. It cannot be shown that this truth and this honorableness, and the intellectual emanations which proceed in accordance with them, are absent when the apprehending, affirming, and loving are infinite, as in the case of God (Lonergan 1964b, 80–83).

It is worth noting that, as Lonergan points out, this method of adverting to the operations of our own minds in order to achieve some understanding of the Trinity is the same as that of Aquinas. Although Aquinas did not explicitly and systematically practise introspection in the manner of some modern authors, he did resolve a number of fundamental problems by appeal to persons' experience of their own mental processes.[5] With regard to the present question, Aquinas remarks that when we attend to our understanding and its operations, we make three discoveries. First, whenever we come to understand anything, because of our very act of understanding, something comes forth within us, namely, the conception of the thing which is understood.[6] Second, by its very nature, love proceeds from and in

---

[4] Lonergan has summarised his understanding of the Trinity as "three subjects of a single dynamic and existential consciousness" (Lonergan 1974, 25). It is supposed to be "dynamic" in that understanding gives rise to judgment, "existential" in that love proceeds accordingly. For an informal exploration of the analogy, see Meynell 1976b.

[5] Thus Aquinas' main argument against the Averroists, who maintained that the "active intellect" is numerically one and the same in all men, is that it is *this particular man* who understands (*Summa contra Gentes*, II, 77, 5; cf. Lonergan 1974, 53); only on the assumption that Averroism is in this particular false, in fact, is the Averroist himself worth arguing with. And Aquinas distinguished with brilliance and precision between consciousness itself on the one hand, and our investigations into it and the results of these on the other (*Summa Theologica*, I, lxxxvi, 1). For Lonergan's relation to Aquinas on the theory of knowledge, and its application to the doctrine of the Trinity, see above all Lonergan 1968.

[6] *Summa Theologica*, I, xxvii, 1.

accordance with a conception of the understanding.[7] Third, that which comes forth in this manner does not necessarily differ from that *from* which it comes forth. Indeed, the more perfectly it comes forth, the more it is one with that *from* which it comes forth.[8] Once these three points are grasped, and their implications drawn out, the problem of understanding the Trinity in terms of the psychological analogy is virtually solved. The remainder of the problem does not involve further insights, but only the drawing-out of implications of those already gained (Lonergan 1964b, 70, 78–79; 1968, chap. 5).[9]

That there are two divine processions—the Word from the Father, the Spirit from Father and Word together—is an essential part of Catholic belief. It has been the general opinion of traditional Catholic theologians that the two processions are to be conceived on the analogy of intellect and will. That they are to be conceived on the analogy of "inner word" (conception) from speaker, and love from both, seems to have been the opinion of Aquinas, and is supported by Lonergan.[10] All the judgments which we make tend to approach the truth to the extent that they derive from full understanding, and every affection which we express is right and honorable to the extent that it proceeds from a true judgment of what is good. Nor can these two, if they are postulated as being in God, be reduced to one and the same thing. For these two states—to emanate from "inner word" and not to emanate from "inner word"—are contradictorily opposed one to the other, and hence cannot belong to one and the same entity. But, on this account, it is of the nature of Love to emanate from the Word, and it is of the nature of the Word to emanate not from itself, but from divine understanding and speaking (Lonergan 1964b, 93, 95).

Lonergan remarks that in the case of human consciousness, truth in judgment about something and a proper emotional attitude towards it are often at one another's expense. People who are good at forming an accurate conception of things, but are not emotionally involved with what they know—who are "intellectuals" in the slightly abusive sense—have the reputation of being somewhat cold. On the other hand, the lover's preoccupation with the object of love is notoriously apt to be at odds with a just conception of it, and it is not for nothing that it is said that love is blind. But Lonergan insists that neither defect is inevitable, since blindness may be overcome

---

[7] Ibid., 3.

[8] Ibid., 1.

[9] If Lonergan's interpretation of these texts of Aquinas is correct, the standard translations are rather unhelpful. The originals are as follows: (i) Quicumque enim intelligit, ex hoc ipso quod intelligit, procedit aliquid intra ipsum, quod est conceptio rei intellectae, et ex vi intellectiva proveniens, et ex eius notitia procedens (ii) . . . de ratione amoris est, quod non procedit nisi a conceptione intellectus (iii) id quod procedit ad intra processu intelligibili, non oportet esse diversum: immo quantum perfectius procedit, tanto magis est unum cum eo a quo procedit.

[10] *Summa Theologica*, I, xcii, 6: ". . . cum increata Trinitas distinguatur secundum processionem Verbi a dicente, et amoris ab utroque."

through clarity of conception at the same time as coldness is dispelled through intensity of love. It is in this state, he suggests, that human consciousness most fully reflects the divine life of which it is the created analogue (Lonergan 1964b, 100–1).

The Catholic doctrine that one cannot prove by natural reasoning that there must be a Word in God has already been alluded to; why the doctrine is correct must now be explained. There are a number of reasons why "inner words" are necessary for human beings. We need them to frame definitions and to concoct theories, and we need them to come to know the truth about the world by apprehending evidence for the applicability of the definitions and theories. In fact, without "inner words", we could never come to know the world in the kind of way that we do, and would be confined to experience and imagination to the exclusion of understanding and judgment. None of these reasons why human beings must make use of "inner words" need apply to God. The divine intellect is not brought into action by means of anything else, in the way that the human intellect is by sense perception, when a puzzling set of data provokes us to the attempt to understand. Indeed, since God eternally knows everything, God's understanding is not subject to any kind of development whatever, by which it could advance from ignorance to knowledge. God exists in infinite and unrestricted perfection, at once understanding God, and understanding all else that exists in and through God, as what God perfectly understands and infallibly wills (Lonergan 1964b, 105–6).[11]

One might object that, to judge by these human parallels, the divine understanding could not be clear or distinct unless it was expressed in "inner words." Lonergan answers that although understanding of the human type, which develops through a series of distinct acts, cannot be clear and distinct except so far as it is expressed in "inner words," the same need not apply to understanding by one infinite and unrestricted act. One might further object that the duality of subject and object is of the essence of knowledge, and that, therefore, unless the divine Subject utters a Word, God cannot know God. Lonergan's retort to this is that the presupposition is simply false, and is based on nothing more than that confusion of knowing with looking which is so frequent a source of confusion in our conception of human knowledge. Not only did it make some theologians mistakenly believe that they had found a proof that there must be a divine Word,[12] but it induced the late Jean-Paul Sartre to distinguish the "in-itself" and the "for-itself" in such a way that he could impugn as self-contradictory the notion of a real God who was conscious of self without need of any other.[13] However, as Aquinas pointed out,

---

[11] For the conception of God to be known without special revelation, cf. Lonergan 1957, chap. 19.

[12] Lonergan cites the nineteenth century Catholic theologians A. Günther and A. Rosmini, whose conclusions were condemned by the First Vatican Council.

[13] For Sartre on God, see Manser 1966, 70–71.

the truth in God's knowledge of self does not depend on the conformity between knower and known, which does indeed presuppose duality, but on the absence of difference between them, which does not (Lonergan 1964b, 106).[14]

It is not immediately evident how one may infer that there are three Persons in God from the proposition that there are two processions. There is an intermediate step, that of showing how the two processions yield four relations. That there are four real relations in God was generally agreed by Catholic theologians of the Middle Ages, after the rather unfortunate attempts to deal with the question by Gilbert de la Porrée[15] and Joachim of Flora.[16] Since there is a procession of the Word, it follows that there is a relation between Word and Speaker. The relation of Word to Speaker in God is termed "filiation"; that of Speaker to Word, "paternity." Similarly, there is a relation between the divine Love on the one hand and the divine Speaker and Word on the other who together and inseparably evince it. The relation of Speaker and Word to Love in God is called "active spiration"; the converse relation, of Love to Speaker and Word, "passive spiration." Thus paternity, filiation, active spiration, and passive spiration are the four relations in God (Lonergan 1964b, 115–17).[17]

Lonergan next sets out to show that these four divine relations are "subsistent." What is meant by this term? Not all entities which are said to "be" are said to "be" in the same sense. Some entities, like unicorns and dragons, only "are" in people's imagination. Other entities are merely possible, in that they may be brought into being in certain circumstances; these "can be" rather than strictly speaking "are." Again, there are properties or qualities whose nature it is to be *in* or *of* something rather than strictly speaking to "be." Finally, in addition to all these entities which "are" in a sort of way, in a qualified sense, there are also, and "are" more properly speaking, entities such as minerals, plants, animals, human persons, God, the Father, the Son, and the Holy Spirit. These, since they "are" simply,

---

[14] *Summa Theologica*, I, xvi, 5, Lonergan 1964b, 106.

[15] DS 745.

[16] DS 803–807.

[17] Lonergan employs a technical distinction of traditional Scholasticism, in maintaining that three of the divine relations are "really distinct" from one another (paternity, filiation, and passive spiration), while there is a "notional" but not "real" distinction between the divine substance and the divine relations. There is a notional distinction between X and Y where the concept of X is not the concept of Y, but things notionally distinct may just the same be really identical. For example, there may be no real distinction between the heaviest man at present living in Blackpool and the richest man at present living in Blackpool. They may be one and the same person. But since the expressions "the richest man in Blackpool" and "the heaviest man in Blackpool" do not mean the same, they are notionally distinct. To use the terminology of G. Frege, which is more familiar to modern philosophers, two expressions having different "senses" may have the same "reference". For example, the phrases "the morning star" and "the evening star" have different senses, but the reference of both is the planet Venus. See Geach and Black 1980, 56–78. DS 803.

since they "are" in a primary rather than in one of the qualified senses mentioned, deserve a special appellation; we will term them "subsistents." In the case of each creature, or of God as such, the subsistent thing is distinct from its relatedness to what is other than itself. But in the case of the Persons of the Trinity, who are constituted as such by their mutual relations, Father and paternity, Son and filiation, Spirator (Father and Son as spirating) and active spiration, Spirit and passive spiration, do not really differ (Lonergan 1964b, 119–20).

It is to be noted that there is no real distinction between the divine essence (that which all the Persons have in common) on the one hand and each of the divine relations on the other. This follows from the principle propounded by the Fourth Council of the Lateran against Joachim of Flora, that there is a Trinity and not a quaternity in God.[18] If a real distinction were involved in each case, there would be a quaternity. Also, it may be inferred from the ruling of the Council of Florence that in God all is one where mutual opposition of relations is not involved. Now one may object that real identity is what logicians call a "transitive" relation, that is, a relation R such that when A has the relation R to B, and B has the relation R to C, A cannot but have the relation R to C. (". . . Is taller than . . ." would be an example of a transitive relation in this sense; ". . . is a cousin of . . ." would not.) Of course, it would then follow that the divine Persons could not at the same time each be really identical with, and only notionally distinct from, the divine essence, and each be really distinct from the others. To meet this objection, Lonergan appeals to the distinction noted earlier between those subsistent beings which are and are what they are only in virtue of their relation to something else and those which are and are what they are in themselves. He then concedes that the conclusion would follow where A, B, and C were all subsistent beings of the latter kind, but denies that it would do so in the case where A and C are subsistent beings of the former, B of the latter, kind. Thus one can claim without self-contradiction that the Father and the Son are each of them really identical with the divine essence, are each really the one God, while remaining really distinct from one another.[19]

---

[18] DS 803.

[19] An example may be helpful. The road from Leeds to Burley is really identical with the A 660, and the A 660 is really identical with the road from Burley to Leeds, but it would be a bold person who inferred that the road from Leeds to Burley was really identical with the road from Burley to Leeds. I could not in all cases substitute the phrase "the road from Leeds to Burley" for "the road from Burley to Leeds" without change of sense; for example, in the case of the proposition "The road from Burley to Leeds runs roughly east-south-east," or of the command "Take the road from Burley to Leeds." The classical example is the identity, noted by Aristotle, between change and the bringing about of change on the one hand and change and the undergoing of change on the other (for Aristotle on change, see his *Physics*, Books III and IV). To call a change an action is to refer it to that which brings it about; to call it an undergoing (for want of a better word) is to refer it to that which is changed. An example is the cutting of a piece of wood by an axe, which the axe brings about, and the piece of wood undergoes. This point is

Let us call those subsistent beings which are and are what they are only by virtue of their relation to something else "relative beings"; those which are and are what they are in themselves "absolute beings." How can there be three Persons in one God, three "subsistents" in one "substance"? Lonergan argues that this is logically possible given that there is a case of three "relative beings" and one "absolute being." He concedes that adequate grounds could never be found for a real distinction between different "absolute beings" within one and the same "absolute being," or indeed for a distinction between "relative beings" not mutually opposed. But he denies that there cannot be mutually opposed "relative beings" within one "absolute being." He admits that there is no actual case which is either demonstrable through consideration of creatures or perfectly intelligible to us during the present life, but denies that this entails that there is no case in which we may believe on the authority of divine revelation and which we can understand to a limited extent. For it is an essential tenet of the Catholic faith that while the Father, the Son, and the Holy Spirit are one and the same God, the Father is not the Son, or the Son the Holy Spirit, or the Holy Spirit the Father. And, as is now in the course of being argued, we can gain a fruitful though imperfect understanding of this tenet by recourse to the psychological analogy, and by an expansion of the account of two processions just derived into that of four real relations, and of three Persons (Lonergan 1964b, 143).

Are the subsistent relations in God which have been described really Persons? In order to reply to this question, one must evidently first determine just what is meant by "person." Lonergan distinguishes five distinct though related senses of the term. First, it may simply be a common term to refer to the Father, the Son, and the Holy Spirit. Augustine uses the term in this very open and non-committal sense.[20] Second, it may be provided with a definition. Thus Boethius defines a person as "an individual substance of a rational nature"; Richard of St. Victor, as "an incommunicable existent of divine nature"; Aquinas, as "a distinct subsistent in an intellectual nature."[21] Third, it may be part of a metaphysical theory that attempts to clarify the notion by embedding it in a wider conceptual framework; such metaphysical theories were propounded by Duns Scotus, Cajetan, Suarez, and others. Fourth, a person may be regarded in psychological rather than metaphysical terms, as a conscious subject or centre of consciousness. Fifth, there is the conception of the person as concretely apprehended, as what can have

---

related to our topic in that the same process here is both an action and an undergoing, which are related to one another by mutual opposition. In this case, of course, unlike that of God, what acts and what undergoes are not one and the same being. The axe cuts, and the wood is cut; but it is the one God who as it were acts and undergoes, who begets and is begotten, spirates and is spirated or proceeds (Lonergan 1964b, 141–42).

[20] Augustine, De Trinitate, VII, iv, 7. ML 42, 939.

[21] Cf. Summa Theologica, I, xxix, 2; III, ii, 2. I owe these references to E. L. Mascall. Aquinas does not actually use this phrase, but it appears to capture his position.

personal relations, is to be called "you," is distinct from a mere thing, and is able to communicate with others. What persons are in this last sense is something to be apprehended not in a technical definition, but rather by a judgment of what all are aware of in their individual experience of life (Lonergan 1964b, 153; 1974, 199–200).

One may well wonder whether all these notions have anything in common. What they have in common is that, in their different ways, they are all answers to the one question, "What is a person?" The following example may be useful by way of illustration. According to Aristotle fire is one of the four elements, while according to modern chemists it is a kind of chemical process. But though these *answers* to the question "What is fire?" are very different from one another, at least the question to which they are proposed as answers is the same. In both cases one is trying to establish *the nature of* X, where X is some sensible phenomenon.[22] The question, asked with reference to determinate data or determinate alleged truths—the former in the case of the natural and human sciences, the later in the case of theology—constitutes a heuristic structure which remains the same whatever the differences between the particular answers that are given (Lonergan 1964b, 154).

Once this point is grasped, as Lonergan says, it is quite simple to see how the five conceptions of a person mentioned above are related to one another. In Augustine, where the notion of person is simply that of whatever there are three of in the Trinity, the conception is open and heuristic, inviting further questions and answers, but with no determinate answer explicitly stated or even implicitly assumed. In Boethius, Richard of St. Victor, and Aquinas attention has shifted to the question "What is a person?", and a direct answer is given to the question. But the definitions which they propounded cannot be clearly and distinctly conceived, or compared with one another and evaluated, unless one has determined, by the asking and answering of further questions, exactly what is meant by the terms "intellectual," "nature," "substance," "incommunicable," and so on. This further step was taken by Scotus, Cajetan, and Suarez in their metaphysical accounts of the nature of a person. Many metaphysical theories were put forward, dealing with other matters as well as this, and since the differences between them seemed irreconcilable, it is no wonder that philosophers from Descartes onwards tended to transfer their attention to what they felt to be prior questions about the nature, scope, and limits of human thought. And when everything else was treated with this psychological bias, it was only natural so to treat the concept of the person. Unfortunately, mutually irreconcilable theories of knowledge have come to proliferate, just as mutually irreconcilable metaphysical theories had previously done. Thus recent authors, typified by the existentialists, have thought it best to abstain from general and

---

[22] For inquiries into "the nature of," see Lonergan 1954, chap. 2.

abstract speculation and to stick to the concrete facts of life. On their view of the matter, the more one lives as a person among persons, the more clearly one understands what is meant by the term. Anyone who can say "I," and to whom "You" can properly be said, is a person; in contrast with what should be referred to as "it," and is not a person but a thing (Lonergan 1964b, 154–55).

In the light of what has been said, Lonergan argues that what we have here is not simply a collection of different opinions about the nature of the person, but a single heuristic structure evolving over time, and differing according to the succession of points of view from which the question "what is a person?" may be asked. That "persons" are what there are three of in the Trinity was presupposed by those who tried to define "person," and definitions of "person" were in turn presupposed by those who tried to work out metaphysical systems to justify and accommodate them. This metaphysical search for the ultimate nature of things is quite consistent with, and may actually be helped on by, a psychological investigation of the human subject, and such investigations are by no means irreconcilable with attention to human subjects in their concrete actions and interrelations. Obviously an exhaustive account of these matters is not relevant to our present purposes. But, as Lonergan remarks, it is worth noting that the Father, the Son and the Holy Spirit are "persons" in all five of the senses distinguished—in name, according to an adequate definition of the person, in metaphysical constitution, in respect to consciousness, and with regard to their relations both with one another and with us. "Person" is the accepted term for what there are three of in God, and in accordance with the Thomist definition, a person is a distinct subsistent in an intellectual nature. In metaphysical terms, as has already been argued, a divine Person is either a subsistent relation or a being distinct by virtue of relation. In psychological terms, a divine Person is a distinct subject conscious of self both as a subject and as distinct. Furthermore, the divine Persons are not only related to one another, as are human persons, by interpersonal relations, but they are constituted as individuals and as Persons by means of them (Lonergan 1964b, 160).

One may object that the Fathers and the great Scholastic theologians were not in the habit of speculating about consciousness in God. But Lonergan retorts that it can hardly be disputed that Christians, whether sophisticated or not, have always worshipped God and each of the divine Persons with the assumption that they are conscious, even if this assumption is not usually spelled out. And when the faithful assume something as a matter of course, it is up to the systematic theologian to indicate clearly and distinctly how it can be so. It is evident that there are a number of difficulties raised by the explicit attribution of consciousness to the divine Persons. If one holds that there are as many consciousnesses[23] as Persons in God, as

---

[23] I am afraid that "consciousnesses" is a somewhat barbarous plural form, but I have been unable to think of a better alternative.

seems a not unnatural assumption, one is forced to the conclusion that there are either three consciousnesses and three Gods, or one consciousness and one Person—in other words, with the heresies of Tritheism or Sabellianism. Similarly, in Christology, one ends up either as a Monophysite or as a Nestorian, with Christ as either one consciousness or two persons. Lonergan solves both problems by drawing a distinction between a consciousness on the one hand and a subject who is conscious on the other. Thus the Persons of the Trinity would be three subjects of a single consciousness; Christ, a single subject of a divine and a human consciousness. Lonergan admits that people may cavil at this preoccupation with "subjects" and the subjective, on the ground that there is a kind of emphasis on subjectivity which leads inevitably to liberalism, modernism,[24] or some other position incompatible with that assent to objective truth which is of the essence of Catholic faith. But it is quite a different matter to vindicate claims to "objective" truth by illustrating and confirming it, as Lonergan sets out to do, by reference to concrete, living, and "subjective" experience. This kind of attention to what is "subjective," he insists, is by no means incompatible with the "objectivity" proper to Catholic belief. On the contrary, it helps to explain and to corroborate it (Lonergan 1964b, 160).

Despite the parallels between divine and human persons, the term "Person" is not used in exactly the same sense in the two cases. In terms of the distinction drawn earlier, human persons differ numerically with respect to "absolute" being as well as to "relative" being; this is not the case with the divine Persons. In the case of God as well as of ourselves, consciousness is acquaintance on the part of subjects with themselves and their acts. But in us this acquaintance is in the first instance inchoate and elementary. It is a necessary *precondition* of our *coming to know* ourselves clearly, distinctly, and (in one sense) objectively, but in itself it lacks the clarity, distinctness, and objectivity of knowledge properly so called. However, in God there is no act which is preliminary to another, and consequently no advance by a series of conscious acts from thought which is obscure and confused to that which is clear and distinct. Such development would be incompatible with the eternity and perfection of God (Lonergan 1964b, 189).

The divine consciousness is one. For it is necessary that consciousness is one where, from an unrestricted understanding, there is once and eternally uttered an unique Word, and where from that understanding and Word there is once and eternally evinced an unique act of Love. But although this divine consciousness is one, each of the divine Persons possess it in a manner peculiar to self. Consciously to "beget," and consciously to be "begotten," and consciously to be "spirated," in the senses determined through the psychological analogy, are distinct from one another. Thus Lonergan con-

---

[24] DS 3475–3500. Modernism, which flourished at the turn of the nineteenth and twentieth centuries, tried to bring Roman Catholic doctrine into what was felt to be greater harmony with contemporary social ideas, science, philosophy, and historiography.

cludes that the one divine consciousness is possessed by the three Persons each in a different manner (Lonergan 1964b, 191).

It is to be noted that the processions from which derive the relations constitutive of the divine Persons are analogous to what is best in human consciousness. For there is nothing higher or more admirable within human consciousness than to be intellectually constrained to assent to what is so, and morally obliged to embrace what is good. In fact, the intellectual consciousness of the human being is simply an imperfect and distant image of those intellectual emanations through which the Son is begotten by the Father and the Holy Spirit is spirated or proceeds from both. In us there are many acts of understanding and few of them adequate; many "inner words" of conception and judgment, and not all of them corresponding to the truth; many expressions of love and by no means all of them appropriate or honorable. But God is a single, perfect, and unrestricted act of understanding, who forms a single and perfect conception of self, from and through which God evinces a single and unsullied act of love (Lonergan 1964b, 192–93).

Of course human persons in their temporality and divine Persons in their eternity are different in many respects. An eternal subject is immutable, a temporal subject undergoes change. The "now" of an eternal subject is always the same, the "now" of a temporal subject, fluid and inconstant. Human subjects, again, each have a sensitive as well as an intellectual consciousness; however, they are capable of intellectually ordering their sensitive living so far as their conception of themselves is just, and their moral attitude towards themselves in accordance with such a just conception.

There are a number of ways in which temporal subjects can develop authentically over time. First, they may gain a clear view of their own intellectual and moral nature—either in common-sense or in systematic terms, according to the differentiation of consciousness which they have achieved—and set themselves to follow its exigences. Second, they may fail to gain such a clear view, but may believe the words of another who does so, and so ultimately come to do so on their own account. Third, the temporal subject may become so united to another in love, that this issues in acceptance of the words of that other, and so ultimately in understanding (Lonergan 1964b, 198–200).[25]

However, the kind of authentic development just described, which happens in accordance with justified conception and honorable affection, encounters many hindrances in the fallen state. As Lonergan says, human beings are disposed to learn only about what relates to the immediate utility and comfort of the present life, since error on such matters is quickly shown up by experience for what it is. But what concerns one's basic nature as such,

---

[25] Cf. the striking remarks of Freud on the necessity for patients to love their therapists, if they are to accept from them the truth about their condition (Freud 1933, 372–73).

one's overall task in the present life, and one's ultimate destiny is by no means so readily determined by experience and practice. This is why such matters are left to the speculations of poets, priests, and philosophers, while other people get on with the more pressing business of day-to-day living. Thus uncultured people tend to fall under the sway of myth, and although the progress of the arts and sciences provides better opportunity for human beings to look into their own nature and discover the immanent norms of its development, at the same time it multiplies pretexts for confusion and aberration on the matter (Lonergan 1964b, 200–1).

But Lonergan adds that of course not only ignorance but also absence of good will must be taken into account. We are liable to prefer the facile persuaders to whose who try to speak the truth as they see it. We are liable to prefer the company of friends who live for pleasure than that of those who sincerely try to lead a good life. So it is that the majority of people either spontaneously go or are willingly led astray. They hardly know what a human being ought to be, and when they do get a glimpse of the truth, they certainly do not wish to shape their lives accordingly. But what human beings are potentially, yet actually only intermittently if at all—conscious subjects who conceive and affirm truly, and love and therefore direct their lives in accordance with such true conception and affirmation—God is infinitely and eternally in the generation of the Son by the Father, and in the spiration of the Holy Spirit by Father and Son together (Lonergan 1964b, 202–4).

From discussion of the Persons we come to that of the "missions," in which divine Persons are "sent" to humankind for its salvation. According to the New Testament and the Christian tradition at large, God the Father "sends" the Son, and Father and Son together "send" the Holy Spirit, in such a way that the Persons sent come to be present in a special manner within creation. It must now be shown how the doctrine of the divine missions is founded on that of the Trinity. First of all, what *is* a divine mission? It is nothing else, Lonergan explains, but a divine relation of origin (being begotten or spirated) together with a suitable concomitant contingent effect within the world of creatures. When dealing with what is stated contingently of God or of one or other divine Person as divine, two things have principally to be borne in mind. Nothing real or intrinsic is added thereby to God or the divine Person in question as divine; but the statement cannot be true without the occurrence of the suitable concomitant effect in question.

To take a parallel example, if it is true that God creates light, nothing is thereby added to God (God does not become greater or more divine by doing so), but light cannot but exist. The missions of the Son and of the Spirit are contingent facts—since, absolutely speaking, there might have been no creation at all, and in that case there could not have come about the incarnation and the sanctification which are the concomitant contingent effects involved in the missions of the Son and the Spirit to creatures. In the case of the Incarnation, the concomitant contingent effect is the coming into existence of a non-subsistent human nature (not *a man*, but rather *manhood*, is assumed by the Son, so that the Son *becomes* a man.)[26] In the case of the bestowal of the Spirit, the concomitant contingent effect is the bringing of already existing human beings into a new and better state (the making of them just and pleasing to God [Lonergan 1964b, 216, 218, 226–27, 232, 234.])[27] In the traditional technical terms of Catholic theology, this state is known as "sanctifying grace;" speaking in terms of interiority and religious experience, Lonergan prefers to allude to "God's gift of his love."[28]

First, the *fact* of the missions must be established from the sources of revelation. Did God the Father send his Son to redeem the human race? The New Testament clearly teaches that he did,[29] and the Gospel of John does so with special frequency.[30] The Son who is sent neither teaches his own doctrine[31] nor seeks his own will;[32] he teaches the doctrine and seeks the will of the Father who sent him. The Son is sent out of the love of the Father[33] for the salvation of the world,[34] that human beings may have life through him,[35] that they may believe and know the Father who sends and the Son who is sent,[36] and so have eternal life.[37] And this mission of the Son has an extension. As the Father sends the Son, so the Son sends the apostles.[38] Moreover, whoever accepts those whom the Son sends, accepts the Son, and whoever accepts the Son, accepts the Father who sent him.[39]

Do the Father and Son send the Holy Spirit? Lonergan insists that this mission is clearly taught in Scripture, though he admits that it is not as frequently referred to as the other. God sends the Spirit of his Son into human hearts,[40] in the name of the Son,[41] and the Paraclete, the Spirit of truth, is sent by the Son.[42] The Holy Spirit is said to be given,[43] to be

---

[26] See pp. 105–11, 114–17 below.

[27] Lonergan 1964b, 216, 218, 226–27, 232, 234. The phrase "concomitant contingent effect" is equivalent to Lonergan's *conveniens terminus ad extra*.

[28] For God's gift of love, see Lonergan 1972, *passim*. For the relationship between this gift and sanctifying grace, see especially 288–89 of that work.

[29] Cf. Gal. 4:4.

[30] John 3:16–17, 8:16, 14:24, 20:21.

[31] John 7:16, 18, 8:28, 12:49, 14:24.

[32] John 4:34, 5:30, 6:38, 8:29.

[33] John 3:16; 1 John 4:9.

[34] John 3:17.

[35] 1 John 4:9.

[36] John 6:29, 11:42, 17:8, 21, 23, 25.

[37] John 5:24, 17:3.

[38] John 17:18, 20:21.

[39] John 13:20; cf. Matt. 10:40, Luke 10:16. Lonergan 1964b, 222.

[40] Gal. 4:6.

[41] John 14:26.

[42] John 15:26.

[43] John 14:16, Rom. 5:5, I Thess. 4:8.

received,[44] to inhabit,[45] to be poured out,[46] and to be a pledge of our inheritance.[47] As in the case of the Son, the Spirit does not set forth her own teaching.[48] Of course, Christ and the Spirit belong closely together. Paul, when speaking of the divine Persons dwelling in and among men, easily shifts from the Spirit to Christ, speaking apparently interchangeably of their dwelling within the faithful.[49]

What is the object of the missions? The mission of the Son comes about so that human beings may be adopted as children, and because we are thus adopted as children, God has sent the Spirit. How is this "sending" to be understood? Lonergan insists that it cannot imply a literal movement from place to place, since all the divine Persons are both incorporeal and omnipresent. He concedes that it may be quite appropriate to *imagine* the Son or the Holy Spirit coming down from the sky. Nonetheless, what is at issue, as he says, is the question of how the divine missions are to be *understood* as opposed to vividly pictured. The Son is sent to restore[50] and to reconcile[51] all things, to the end that God may be all in all.[52] The Spirit is sent not with a view to the performance of this or that particular act, but to be the principle of Christian living in each individual human person. The fulfilment of both missions involves human cooperation. As Augustine said, "He who created you without your playing a part, will not so justify you."[53] The basic clue to a proper understanding of the missions, according to Lonergan, is that they are a matter of an entering into and confirming of new personal relations between God and human beings. The mutual love commended by the Son,[54] and the intimate personal relations by which human beings come to belong to one another and to God rather than to themselves, pertain especially to the mission of the Spirit (Lonergan 1964b, 240–41).[55]

The final end of both missions is the same—that new relations of mutual knowledge and love may be established between God the Father and all human persons. It may be asked what kind of benefits accrue to humanity as a result of the divine missions, and how do they come into being. Lonergan explains that, in addition to the good that is constituted by the satisfaction of particular human desires and needs, there is a good of order in human affairs, which ensures the systematic realisation of such desires and needs. (Examples of the good of order are an efficiently-run economy and a just

---

[44] John 20:22, Rom. 8:15, Gal. 3:2.
[45] Rom. 8:9, 11, 1 Cor. 3:16, 6:19.
[46] Acts 2:17, Tit. 3:6.
[47] Eph. 1:14.
[48] John 16:33.
[49] Rom. 8:9–10.
[50] Eph. 1:10.
[51] Col. 1:20.
[52] 1 Cor. 15:28.
[53] Augustine, *Sermon* 169, 11.
[54] John 15:9–10.
[55] 1 Cor. 6:19, Rom. 5:5, Eph. 4:30.

political system.) Now all good of order is a matter to be grasped by understanding rather than merely to be apprehended by sensation or feeling, and it is therefore no wonder that we only gradually come to conceive, want, and work for it.

Lonergan points out that for the good of order to exist within any group of human beings, from a family to a nation state, a number of conditions have to be met. The members of the group must on the whole be disposed to want and work for the same goals, and each must act for them in a way which is to some degree coordinated with the action of all the rest. For this to be possible, there must be personal relations of mutual knowledge and affection between the members of the group. When we love someone, we want to share with him or her the good things that we have. And the more we cooperate with one another to this end, the more we tend to develop the habits and skills which are of assistance in bringing this end about. So it is that once union in love with a community is realised, the other preconditions of the good of order will tend to follow in its train. The most obvious case in point is the successful marriage (Lonergan 1964b, 244–46).[56]

The ultimate end of the missions of the Son and of the Spirit is our direct contemplation of God in heaven, which is the highest of all goods possible for human beings; their proximate end is a good of order within human society. This good of order is referred to in various ways in Scripture, by analogy with other examples of the good of order, as the Kingdom of God, the body of Christ, the Church or community, the mystical marriage of Christ with the Church, the economy of salvation, and the city of God. The implied comparisons are obviously with a political order, the order of a living organism, a social order, a domestic order, and an order promoting the production and distribution of material goods. Lonergan points out that in the case of the community inaugurated by the divine missions, each of the characteristics of the good of order which were mentioned above are to be found. Many persons are involved, since Christ died for all, and many acknowledge his Lordship. There is the common purpose of "putting off the old man" and "putting on the new", and the combined efforts of Christians in doing this for themselves and assisting others in doing it. There is a series of particular goods—the fruit borne continually through the new life in Christ, the ministry of the Word whereby the gospel is preached to every creature, the administration of the sacraments, and the hierarchy which (at least when it functions as it should) provides structure and cohesion within the community. Last but by no means least, there are personal relations of mutual knowledge and affection, when Christians love one another as Christ loved them,[57] and loving one another love Christ,[58] and loving Christ are loved by

---

[56] On the last point, see "Finality, Love, Marriage" (Lonergan 1967, 16–53).
[57] John 13:34, 15:12.
[58] Matt. 25:31–46.

the Father,[59] and have the Spirit conferred upon them through Christ. Every good of order is in some way an imitation of the supreme good of order to be found within the Trinity itself. But the economy of salvation, whose object is a sharing by creatures in the divine beatitude, not only *imitates* this order but also, as a result of the missions, actually *participates* in it (Lonergan 1964b, 246–47).

The just are indwelt by the divine Persons according to the love that is within them, as we find in many places in the New Testament.[60] This indwelling is interpreted by Thomas Aquinas in the following way; that by conferring grace upon them, God comes to be within the just as the known is present within the knower and the beloved present within the lover. Since knowing and loving are characteristic of persons, the mutual presence of those who know and love one another may be called "personal", and it seems that, the greater the good of order within a group of persons, the more intimate is their personal presence to one another. Friends who pursue a common good of order and who cooperate in such a way as to enjoy the particular goods which it entails eventually cease to live for themselves, and come to share a common life. The same applies even more to those who enjoy the fellowship of God in the life of grace. Of course it is true that all creatures are known and loved by God. But some are known and loved by God in a special way, as conformed to the image of God's Son, who is the first-born of many brothers and sisters.[61] They are in a unique manner affirmed in the divine Word through which God affirms both God and everything else which exists, and similarly loved through the divine Love which proceeds from Father and Word together (Lonergan 1964b, 250–53).[62]

---

[59] John 14:21, 16:27.
[60] Cf. John 14:20–21, 17:26; 1 John 4:8, 12, 16.
[61] Rom. 8:29.
[62] Cf. *Summa Theologica*, I, xxxiv, 3.

# Chapter 8

# THE PERSON OF CHRIST

To claim, as orthodox Christians do, that one and the same being is both human and divine, would seem contradictory. After all, to be divine is to be eternal, incorporeal, and immutable; to be human is to be temporal, corporeal, changeable, and liable to suffering. Ultimately, the Church resolved the issue by maintaining that Christ is one Person in two natures.[1] With respect to his divinity he is impassible, immutable, and so on, and with respect to his humanity he is changeable, liable to suffering, and the rest (Lonergan 1964c, 113–14).

The Arians denied not only the divinity of Christ, but in effect his full humanity as well. They denied that he had a human soul, and they conceived the incarnation strictly as a matter of the union of a soul with a body.[2] An Arian bishop of Constantinople, who died in about 370, put the view neatly in a profession of faith: "We believe . . . in one Lord Jesus Christ . . . incarnate and not inhumanate" *(incarnatum et non inhumanatum)*. (In effect, he was claiming that the Word took upon himself a human *body,* but not *manhood,* which would have included a human consciousness.) Of these three cardinal Arian doctrines, Apollinaris rejected one and retained two. He affirmed the strict divinity of the Word, but he denied that Christ had a human intellect, and he conceived the union of Word and flesh strictly on the analogy of that of soul and body in a human being. Apollinaris laid particular stress on the Scriptural phrase "in the likeness of men."[3] The result is that for him Christ is consubstantial with us in respect of his body but not of his soul, and consubstantial with God in respect of his soul but not of his body (Lonergan 1964c, 106–7, 109).

Now it does seem clear that, on the New Testament account, Jesus really was a man, whatever else he may have been. The account states that this man[4] prayed,[5] advanced in wisdom,[6] was obedient,[7] learned obedience

---

[1] DS 302.

[2] That the Arians held that the pre-existent Word took the place of the human soul in Christ as man is stated by Epiphanius, Nemesius, Theodore of Mopsuestia, and Cyril of Alexandria.

[3] Phil. 2:7.

[4] Acts 2:22, 17:31.

[5] Mark 1:35, 6:46, 14:35, 39; etc.

[6] Luke 2:40, 52.

[7] Phil. 2:8, Rom. 5:19.

through suffering,[8] and offered up prayers and petitions with loud cries and tears.[9] These are actions of a being with human thoughts and emotions, and not those of a mere divinity clothed in human flesh. The Fathers also used against the Apollinarists the argument that whatever in human nature is not assumed by Christ is not restored by him. Gregory of Nyssa teaches that Christ rose from the dead "so that remaining in both parts of his nature exhibiting the properties of both, he might save the nature of bodies through his body and the nature of souls through his soul."[10] The Council of Chalcedon stated that the Word became incarnate by uniting himself not merely to the *body* of a man, but to a human body animated by a human soul (Lonergan 1964c, 105, 110–12).

In approaching the history of this question, Lonergan insists on the importance of distinguishing between the substantive and the merely terminological differences of those who disputed over it. He also points out the diverse conceptual schemas which they employed. At Alexandria, theologians employed what may be called a "Word-flesh" schema, while a "man-God" schema prevailed at Antioch. The Word-flesh schema does not direct attention to the human soul, intellect, and will of Christ, but it does facilitate conception of his real unity; whereas the man-God schema has just the opposite merits and disadvantages. Thus Cyril of Alexandria, in his earlier works, is silent about the human thoughts and emotions of Christ.[11] He speaks of the "one incarnate nature of the Word of God," and explains that there are no more two natures than two Sons. When objections were raised against this formula, Cyril admitted both that Christ had a human soul and that there were two natures before the incarnation, yet he still denied that there remained two natures in Christ after the incarnation (Lonergan 1964c, 119).

Cyril's Second Letter to Nestorius, which was approved by the Council of Ephesus,[12] explains how the eternal Word could have suffered, died, and risen from the dead. It was not, Cyril wrote, the divine nature itself which suffered and was wounded, since that nature is impassible. But, since the eternal Word had taken a human body as his own, he suffered and died in that body, for the impassible was in a body capable of suffering. Nestorius had cited many texts of Scripture to show that the suffering, and more particularly the birth, of Christ pertained not to his divinity but to his humanity, and he inferred from this interpretation that the Virgin Mary was strictly speaking not the God-bearer but the Christ-bearer. However, Cyril's letter insists that it is *one and the same* who is both the eternal Word and a man who suffered, died, and rose again. Because he maintains that the man

---

[8] Heb. 5:8.
[9] Heb. 5:7.
[10] *Antirrheticus adv. Apollinarium*.
[11] E.g., in the *Thesaurus* and *Dialogues*.
[12] DS 250–268.

Jesus and God the Son are one and the same, Cyril can argue that the mother of Jesus is the Mother of God. Nestorius was quite right to maintain that Christ suffered in his humanity but not in his divinity, and that his birth from Mary was the birth not of his divinity but of his humanity. But the crucial question is, *who* has this divinity and humanity. What is implied by the Nicene Creed, emphasised by Cyril, and evaded by Nestorius, is this: he who before time began was the Son of God, himself in time became man, suffered, died and rose again (Lonergan 1964c, 123–24, 126, 128–30; 1974, 253–60).

Lonergan admits that the doctrine that there is one person in Christ, and that a divine one,[13] may mislead some who rightly insist that Christ was a real human person. They may well ask whether the statement that the one person in Christ is divine, and that the human nature is personless, does not conflict with his true humanity. The trouble here is a certain ambiguity in the concept "person." To *be* a human person, in the modern sense, is to have a human body and real human thoughts and feelings, and that Christ was a human person in this sense is implied by the doctrine that he was truly man, that he had a real human nature. But for Christ to have *had* a human person as well as a divine person, in the sense of "person" at issue in the Patristic era, would imply that it was someone other than the eternal Son who acted, spoke, thought, and felt as the Gospels tells us that Jesus did (Lonergan 1974, 254, 259–60).[14]

When these developments, together with the questions which gave rise to them and the conceptual schemas within which they were considered, are taken into account, one is in some position to answer anyone who states, or even implies, that the Fathers set aside the teachings of the Gospel in favor of metaphysical speculations about "nature," "person," "substance," and the rest. In general, as Lonergan says, this sort of objection overlooks the fact that what is affirmed within one social and cultural milieu has to be reformulated in order to make sense in another such milieu.[15]

Oscar Cullmann, for example, excludes from Christology all considerations relating to "person" or "nature."[16] No one can possibly disagree with him so far as he is writing simply as an interpreter of the New Testament authors who attempts to recover their viewpoint, and hence engages in the second functional specialty. They nowhere speak of "person" or "nature" in any sense remotely resembling that at issue in the declarations of the relevant Greek councils. But apparently this is not the only matter with which Cullmann is concerned. He maintains that the Christology of the New Testament is strictly functional, and that for this reason the sort of develop-

---

[13] DS 554.

[14] "The meaning of the term 'Person' at Chalcedon is not what commonly is understood by the term today, and theologians at least have to take that fact into account" (Lonergan 1974, 260).

[15] Cf. pp. 20–24 above.

[16] Cullmann 1957, 9, 198, 243, 273, 300, 304, 336–37.

ment imposed upon it by the Fathers is illegitimate. But, as Lonergan points out, this seems to neglect the very possibility of what he himself is at pains to argue, that one claim can be made from a number of different viewpoints, and that what Christ is "for us" may have important implications for what he actually is in himself. (Could Christ properly "function" as divine with respect to us, if he were not actually divine?) If some philosophical assumption is in the background of Cullmann's contention, Lonergan wonders whether the philosophy concerned has an adequate grasp of the nature of truth (Lonergan 1964c, 116, 144).

The seventh century saw another important evolution in Christological doctrine. Chalcedon had determined that there was in Christ one person, and two natures each of which retained its own properties (which is to say, of course, that Jesus Christ was one individual who was both human and divine, without either his humanity or his divinity being modified or compromised). The implications were now spelled out for the operations and the wills of Christ. The fundamental principle to be observed is that set out by Maximus the Confessor and John Damascene:[17] "Operations are *of* the person *from* the nature." Once one has grasped this principle, it becomes clear that the Monophysites, who acknowledge but one nature in Christ, should in consistency affirm one operation and one will, and that those who conform to the Council of Chalcedon, and acknowledge two natures in Christ, must infer that there are two operations and two wills. Those who claimed to accept the Council of Chalcedon, but did not admit two operations and two wills in Christ, were not really consistent. Given that Christ is both God and man, he must operate and will as such, and consequently have two operations and two wills (Lonergan 1964c, 193–95).

It may be seen that there were a number of steps in the evolution of the doctrine of Christ's person and natures, which took nearly three centuries altogether. The first step was the achievement of the school of Antioch, which established that there were two natures in Christ. Diodorus of Tarsus, however, so emphasised the distinction between them that the unity of Christ's person could not be accounted for. And this defect in the Antiochene position was what led to the Nestorian heresy. The second step was taken by Cyril of Alexandria, who affirmed with the utmost clarity and emphasis the unity of the Person who eternally is the Word of God and in time became a man. The third step was taken by Pope Leo I and the Antiochene theologians who formulated the doctrine of one person in two natures. The fourth step was due mainly to the errors of the "monenergites" and the "monothelites," who held respectively that there was one operation and one will in Christ; these impelled the orthodox to stipulate that he had two operations and two wills.

In brief, the whole development amounts to this. What is said about

---

[17] MG 90, 152B; MG 95, 165.

Christ in the New Testament is said either about more than one being or about one and the same being. If it is said about one and the same being, then if it is not contradictory, it cannot be said about him in the same respect. The solution is that it is said in respect either of his divine or his human nature, properties, operation or will. From an orthodox Christian viewpoint the development is to be ascribed ultimately to Divine providence, which, as Lonergan suggests, *could have* willed a universe in which there was neither evil nor error, but which *did* will a universe in which both evils and errors are permitted, so that greater good may come about through the overcoming of the evil and that truth may be known ever more clearly through the repudiation of error (Lonergan 1964c, 203, 205, 207–8).

So much for a summary of the process from *dialectics* through *foundations* to *doctrines* in Christology, and of the reasons why it is appropriate for religiously, morally, and intellectually converted subjects, given that they accept the existence of God and God's special revelation in the New Testament, to assent to the doctrine that Christ is one Person in two natures, with all its consequences. What problems do these conclusions create for *systematics?* How is the doctrine to be justified in terms of a metaphysics based on interiority? Lonergan's fundamental claim is this. The doctrine that Christ is one Person in two natures is to be understood as implying that he is one subject of two types of consciousness, a human and a divine (Lonergan 1974, 25).

Only recently have theologians come to be concerned explicitly with the problem of the consciousness of Christ. Thus it is hardly surprising that they disagree about the matter. P. Galtier would have it that there was in Christ, apart from the divine Person, a human psychological subject, and that this subject knew the divine Person through the beatific vision which he enjoyed. In a somewhat similar vein, L. Seiller wrote: "God the Word is the adored subject and not at all the adoring subject, the subject who is prayed to and not at all the subject who prays" (Seiller 1939, 17).[18] Such views smack suspicously of Nestorianism transposed into a psychological key, compromising as they appear to do the unity of the Person of Christ. Some pronouncements of the *magisterium* of the Catholic Church seem to be directed against such opinions (Lonergan 1964c, 269–70).[19]

We should remember that it is basic to Lonergan's position to distinguish sharply between a theory of knowledge which conceives it on the analogy of taking a look, and a truly critical, and correct, theory which conceives it as a matter of experience, understanding, and judgment. Each theory has its psychological counterpart. On one view, we take a sort of inner look at our conscious selves, just as the naive realist takes an outer look at the things of the world and mistakes it for knowledge. In effect, consciousness is con-

---

[18] Cf. Galtier 1939, 1947; Lonergan 1956, 138–40.
[19] CF. DS 3905.

ceived on the analogy of perception. This account, persistent as it is in human thought, leads into notorious paradoxes when it is consistently applied. (Like David Hume and Bertrand Russell, we may be driven to the conclusion that we are not selves or conscious subjects, but only bundles of "perceptions" or sense-data, just because the "inner look" does not reveal a conscious subject or self.)[20] And when applied to Christology it leads to insoluble anomalies and paradoxes. One is faced with a pseudo-problem about how the human nature can have a perception of the divine, or the divine of the human, and no satisfactory solution can or could possibly be forthcoming. Lonergan remarks sardonically that the nonsensical proposal that Christ is ontologically one but psychologically two does not really mend matters.

On the other view, the one defended by Lonergan, all of us, as human subjects, are conscious or aware both of ourselves and of our acts of sensation, feeling, inquiring, understanding, marshalling evidence, judging, deliberating, deciding, and so on. As our sense-experience is the basis for our knowledge of the external world, so our awareness of ourselves and of our conscious acts is the basis for that knowledge of ourselves which may be expressed in an adequate psychological or cognitional theory. Lonergan claims that this account of consciousness is both satisfactory in itself and the basis for some measure of understanding of the mystery of the Incarnation (Lonergan 1956, 147). The solution to the problem of the consciousness of Christ is that one and the same Word of God is conscious of, or present to, himself in two ways, a human and a divine.

What is meant by "present to himself" in this context? Evidently merely local presence, the sense in which one material object might be said to be "present to" another, is not at issue. Lonergan explains that the kind of "presence to" involved is that which is peculiar to beings capable of consciousness, to "persons" in the common or garden sense as contrasted with mere "things." This kind of self-presence is absent from one who is in deep sleep, begins when one dreams, and increases to a marked extent when one wakes up. This self-presence is at an *empirical* level insofar as one enjoys sensations, emotions, and feelings. It rises to a specifically *intellectual* level when one inquires about one's experiences, when one understands, conceives, defines, and propounds theories or hypotheses. It reaches the next or *rational* level when one reflects on what one has understood, inquires into whether one's suppositions are actually so, weighs evidence, and judges in accordance with that evidence. It arrives at the fourth and final or *moral* level with the transition froom true judgment to morally good decision, when one deliberates, chooses, and acts in accordance with what one has judged to be the case (Lonergan 1964c, 271–72)

In accordance with common usage, Lonergan defines beings as "con-

---

[20] David Hume, *A Treatise of Human Nature*, I, iv, 2; Russell 1956, 279.

scious" when they are present to themselves in the manner just described, and to a greater or lesser extent capable of sensation and feeling, intelligent, reasonable, and responsible. As shown in our discussion of the doctrine of the Trinity, Lonergan relies heavily on a distinction between *that which* is conscious and the consciousness *by which* it is conscious, expressing in a psychological mode the medieval scholastic distinction between the subsistent being which *has* the essence or nature, and the essence or nature itself. Conscious subjects are directly aware of those conscious acts by which they are conscious. These acts constitute data for knowledge of themselves, just as the contents of their senses constitute data for their knowledge of the external world. And as in the case of knowledge of the external world, Lonergan emphasizes that the enjoyment of such data is not itself knowledge, which is to be gained through inquiry into experience issuing in understanding and judgment, but is only a *precondition* of knowledge (Lonergan 1964c, 273–75).

As Lonergan sees it, our experience and knowledge of ourselves as conscious subjects has a vital bearing on the theological notion of "Person," and of what it might be for Christ to be one "Person" in two "natures." He admits that if one reads modern accounts of the person, which stress this matter of consciousness, one fails to find there what traditional Christian theologians have to say about the "person" in their theological and metaphysical investigations. From this one might well rashly conclude that modern investigations of consciousness have no bearing on "persons" in the theological sense of the term, let alone on the question of what it might be for a divine Person to have a human as well as a divine nature. But Lonergan insists that the conclusion would be a mistake. Though Duns Scotus and the others did not treat persons from the specifically psychological point of view, it can easily be shown that to approach their work in this way both clarifies the problems with which they were concerned and enables more satisfactory solutions to be found for them. This is of course a rider to Lonergan's general methodological position, that the realms of common sense and theory are clarified, both in themselves and in their relations with one another, by an inquiry based on interiority (Lonergan 1964c, 281–83).

If one transposes the metaphysical issue into psychological terms, one may readily see why it is important for theology to distinguish in the case of Christ between consciousness and the one who is conscious. Otherwise, in preserving the unity of Christ's person, one would be driven to attribute to him a divine consciousness and to deny him a human one, which would be the Monophysite heresy transposed into psychological terms; or else, in the manner of so many modern authors, to deny him a divine nature or consciousness. Alternatively, in the manner of the Nestorians, in order to preserve the two natures or types of consciousness in Christ, one would have to insist on there being two psychological subjects in Christ, a human and a divine. What it comes to is that only on the basis of a distinction between consciousness, on the one hand, and the one who is conscious, on the other, can the systematic theologian avoid Monophysism or Nestorianism (Lonergan 1964c, 284–85).

Lonergan suggests that there are many ordinary examples by which we can grasp to some extent what it is for a single individual to have more than one kind of consciousness. In the case of a single human individual, we do not say that it is one person who sleeps, another who wakes up, a third who is hungry and eats, a fourth who inquires and understands, a fifth who makes decisions, a sixth who acts accordingly, and so on. It is *one and the same* (to use the phrase on which Cyril of Alexandria was so insistent) who is in all these states and performs all these acts. Even if persons become insane for a while, they can later—assuming that they are later restored to sanity—tell us of those things which then seemed real *to them* but which they now know to have been figments of their imagination. All these examples illustrate that there is a distinction to be made between the individual *who* is consciously present to self and the sort of consciousness *by which* that individual is so present (Lonergan 1964c, 285–6).

If any being has two natural and intellectual operations, that being has two modes of consciousness. But it is an article of Catholic faith that Christ has two natural and intellectual operations, an infinite and a finite, unconfusedly and unchangeably.[21] Thus it seems that Christ has two modes of consciousness. To be sure, the divine Word does not fail to be conscious or present to himself, as though he were a stone, a plant, or a sleeping animal. On the contrary, he is far more conscious, more present to himself, than a fully wakeful person or even an angel, since he is really identical with the infinite understanding which is God. The divine Word is conscious and present to himself as divine, and thus in a specifically divine way. As for his human consciousness, the passion of Christ would have been not real but merely apparent, unless he had been conscious and present to himself in a specifically human as well as a specifically divine way. For Catholics cannot say, on pain of heresy, that Christ suffered in his divine nature;[22] or, on pain of talking nonsense, that he somehow suffered in his human nature without actually feeling anything (Lonergan 1964c, 289–92).

Lonergan admits that the account of the person which he is proposing in this context is not quite what is found in the works of psychologists or phenomenologists, though he tries to take their findings into account. This is to say that such authorities are not concerned with theological questions themselves, or with the philosophical and metaphysical problems which are most closely related to these. Thus it is no part of their business to articulate such distinctions as those between a human psychological subject, a merely human psychological subject, and a psychological subject as such. These

[21] DS 557.
[22] DS 166.

distinctions, however, are necessary, as Lonergan sees it, if one is to gain a clear conception of the Catholic doctrine of the person of Christ. Furthermore, if theologians follow contemporary psychologists and phenomenologists blindly, they will inevitably find themselves in one of the positions which have already been argued to be heretical—the denial that Christ has a truly human consciousness or the denial that he has a truly divine consciousness, or the claim that there are two psychological subjects in Christ (Lonergan 1964c, 297).

Some who approach the problem of the consciousness of Christ are inclined to wonder how anything created and human, like Christ as man, can become conscious of a divine Person. But it can easily be seen that, in the light of what has been said, their question is framed the wrong way. *That which* is conscious and present to itself is none other than the divine Person who is the Word, who through the Incarnation became conscious and present to himself in a human as well as in a divine way (Lonergan 1964c, 304).[23]

How, one may ask, is the theory of the two natures in Christ to be applied to the vexed question of his knowledge? As has already been shown at length, if we are to do justice to the teaching of the New Testament as a whole, we must say that the relation in which Jesus stands to God the Father is absolutely unique; it cannot be understood merely on the model of God's relation to the prophets and inspired writers. The whole mystery of Christ consists in the fact that the words and deeds of the man Jesus manifest the divine mystery in an incarnate manner. But to understand this unique relation between Jesus and the Father merely in terms of morality, or of religious feeling, or somehow "ontologically" but in such a way that knowledge is excluded, is to go against the express teaching of the Fourth Gospel. For this speaks quite explicitly of what the Son "sees" and "knows" in the presence of the Father.[24] He who as man uttered to other men the divine mysteries actually *saw* the Father. Thus anyone who denies immediate knowledge of God by Jesus Christ contradicts the teaching of John. Such a claim, as Lonergan says, would imply not only that Christ had no knowledge of the things of which he spoke, but that he did not see and know what, according to John, he did claim explicitly to know and have seen. One should note that the argument in favor of Christ's knowledge based on the Fourth Gospel could also find support in at least one text of the Synoptics,[25] which teaches a mutual and exclusive knowledge by the Father and the Son, on which is founded the authority of the Son as revealer of the Father (Lonergan 1964c, 387–90).

It is to be concluded that, according to the witness of the New Testament, Christ taught the mysteries of God not as though he was ignorant of them,

---

[23] Cf. Gutwenger 1960, 77.
[24] John 3:11, 6:46, 7:29, 8:38, 55, 25.
[25] Matt. 11:27; Luke 10:22.

like other people, but as though he knew them directly. And it is obvious such knowledge on the part of Christ as man is in every way appropriate to what he had to do. His mission was to teach all nations,[26] and it would have been absurd, in this case as in others, for the blind to attempt to lead the blind.[27] And, as Lonergan says, it is necessary for faith ultimately to derive from knowledge, if it is to have any validity. In a case where everyone believes and no one really knows, no one believes with good reason. Christians believe through faith in Christ, who, as they believe, knew divine truth directly, and hence was in a position to tell his followers what to believe (Lonergan 1964c, 391).

In the evolution of the Church's view of Christ's knowledge since New Testament times, three stages are to be distinguished, the patristic, the medieval, and the modern. The Fathers were preoccupied with the question whether Christ, even as man, could be ignorant of anything. In this case as in others, their thought was not developed in an orderly and systematic manner, but was addressed to particular problems which arose in refuting the arguments of heretics, in expounding Scripture, or in vindicating the knowledge on the part of the Son of what he revealed to us. In this as in other matters the medieval theologians accepted the consensus of the Fathers, not merely repeating it, but reformulating it in such a way that it could be expounded and justified in a systematic manner. Little by little they evolved an account of Christ's knowledge which may be summarised as follows. Christ as man had immediate knowledge of God ("blessed" knowledge), and knowledge of every other reality both through the mediation of this and directly by "infused" knowledge. This "infused" knowledge consisted of knowledge of all things in their proper order, in the manner appropriate to the human mind at the term of its development. (His possession of this knowledge was a consequence of the plenitude of grace in him.) In addition to these two kinds of knowledge in Christ, they maintained that he had an "acquired" knowledge obtained in the usual manner by inquiry into sensible particulars.[28] Later Catholic theologians repeated this account faithfully until quite recently (Lonergan 1964c, 353–54).

However, what was once readily accepted by the faithful seems to many people now to be beset by extreme and perhaps insoluble difficulties. Since about the beginning of the nineteenth century, there have been misgivings among Catholics about the accepted account of Christ's knowledge. Some have suggested that the matter is uncertain, that the arguments underlying the received doctrine are of dubious validity, and that the clear statements of Scripture, to the effect that Christ advanced in wisdom[29] and that there were

---

[26] Matt. 28:19.

[27] Matt. 15:14; Luke 6:39.

[28] Cf. *Summa Theologica* III, ix–xii.

[29] Luke 2:52.

limits to what he knew,[30] have been overlooked. Some have complained that direct vision of the divine splendor on the part of Christ as man, as stated by the traditional account, could not be reconciled either with his sufferings or with his merits. Further, it seemed to some that the knowledge of the future entailed by it was incompatible with his freedom of will. Many people of course have resolved the difficulty by denying the divinity of Christ altogether, while others, who set store by the values of Christianity but care little for the detail of its doctrines, have preferred to keep silent about the matter (Lonergan 1964c, 354, 357–58).

Lonergan points out that, in seeking for a solution to this problem, one must note how and why the questions raised by the medieval theologians differ from those raised by theologians of our own times. The former started from the assumption that Christ, being divine, had perfect knowledge, and deduced from that general possibilities for his human knowledge and activity. The latter start from the words, actions, and decisions which make up the human life of Christ, and the human history of which these form a part. It is foolish to maintain that the medievals were wrong in not concerning themselves with the questions which have arisen more recently. On the other hand, one cannot simply set out the answers worked out by the medievals and assume that the more recent problems are sufficiently dealt with. If one wishes to understand and reap the full benefits of the modern point of view, without denying doctrines which have been solemnly defined by the Church, one cannot avoid the arduous intellectual labor conveyed by the slogan *vetera novis augere et perficere* (Lonergan 1964c, 396, 347, 354).[31]

Lonergan proposes that these difficulties can be met, and that the medieval and modern concerns may be encompassed within a single viewpoint, if the following hypothesis is accepted. In addition to the knowledge appropriate to his divine nature, Christ had a human kind of knowledge. This was ineffable as well as effable, and supernatural as well as natural. By means of his ineffable knowledge, which is equivalent to the "blessed" and "infused" knowledge postulated by the medievals, Christ as man knew God immediately, and knew mediately everything required for his mission on earth. But it was his effable knowledge which included that kind of knowing, both natural and supernatural, which made his life a genuinely human and historical one. To say that some of Christ's effable knowledge is "supernatural" is to say that it is of divine mysteries inaccessible to the human mind as such, by the imparting of which to other human beings a "supernatural" way of life is rendered possible for them (Lonergan 1964c, 332, 356).

Let us remember that, on Lonergan's account, human knowledge is

---

[30] Mark 13:52.

[31] "To increase and perfect the old things with the new." This slogan, due to Pope Leo XIII, is seen by Lonergan as summing up his own intellectual aims.

threefold, consisting of experience, understanding, and judgment. Just the same will apply to the effable knowledge of Christ. Divine knowledge, however, consists in a single unrestricted act of understanding, which extends to all actual and possible states of affairs whatever. The effable knowledge characteristic of human beings as such is backed up at every stage by sensation, which provides images to elicit understanding and means to verify or falsify such understanding as has been achieved. Ineffable knowledge, however (of which we can gain some conception from the writings of the mystics), is neither gained through sensation nor readily expressible by concepts closely connected with sensation. (We should bear in mind, of course, that Lonergan employs the term "ineffable" in a technical rather than a rhetorical sense—in the latter of which one might say that a lady's kindness or a colleague's gall was ineffable.) The immediate knowledge of God is ineffable, and is such as is described, so far as it is capable of description, by Paul.[32] It is not through a glass darkly, but face to face, not in part, but even as we are known. Christ as man will have possessed from the first the immediate and ineffable knowledge of God, which is the ultimate goal toward which all other human beings strive. The object of his human living was to express this knowledge in an effable form suitable to persons of that place and time, so that ultimately it could become available to those of other places and times (Lonergan 1964c, 345, 354).

Lonergan is perfectly aware of the objection that such a view is just medieval and outdated, but he suggests that those who reject it out of hand should consider what is fitting to the dignity of the Son's humanity, and what knowledge the Son of man would be liable to have because of his immediate knowledge of God and of the hypostatic union.[33] But that Christ is truly human implies that, while living on earth, he underwent a psychological development appropriate to a human being—the sort of development that has been described so fully in the work of Jean Piaget. It implies that he took upon himself the life not just of an adult but of an infant, that he became an adult through years of experience, of learning and choosing, and that like the rest of us he came step by step to form his own peculiar character, his own way of talking and doing things. However, it also follows from what has been said that he so formed himself not merely through such natural and human conscious acts; nor yet through these assisted by the light of faith, as though he were one of the members of his mystical body and not the head; but that he lived the whole of his life in such a way as to show forth the divine mysteries through the medium of a human life, and the words and acts of which it consisted (Lonergan 1964c, 345, 354).

How is this psychological account of Christ, as one being with two modes

---

[32] 1 Cor. 13:12.
[33] I.e., the union of the divine and human nature in the one Person Jesus Christ.

of consciousness, to be applied to the metaphysical disputes about Christology which have characterised Catholic theology until quite recently?[34] The basic metaphysical problem can be expressed as follows. How is it that the embodied human nature which was born of the Virgin Mary, and which suffered and died under Pontius Pilate, could be one and the same as the eternal Word of God? Must not the historical Jesus, so to say, be an individual complete in himself, like other human beings? Aristotle's doctrine, that number presupposes matter and quantity, has already been mentioned.[35] Its corollary is that what makes a thing of a type *one* thing of that type is material continuity. The sense in this is obvious. Two typewriters, however alike they are, are two by virtue of consisting of distinct parcels of matter. And however much two human beings, say identical twins, resemble one another, they are distinct by virtue of the stuff which makes them up, so that they occupy different segments of space-time.[36]

As has already been argued, not everything which can be said to "be" can be said to "be" in just the same sense.[37] One may distinguish "subsistent being," as that which is the primary sense, from that which is related to it in some way—for example, as essential or accidental properties *of* that which is, as possible things or states of affairs which *are* not but rather *can* be, or as fictitious entities which are not but can be thought about. Lonergan points out that "subsistent being" is one or a unity so far as it is *not* distinct within itself, but *is* distinct from everything else, where "distinct from" is nothing other than what is apprehended in the true judgment "A is not B," where A and B are subsistent beings.

In this connection we must recall Lonergan's account of the essential role of judgment in our apprehension of reality. Unity of subsistent being is to be apprehended in judgment. This leaves open the possibility, not apparently envisaged by Aristotle, that such unity is not necessarily either material unity or unity of essence or nature. Thus unity of essence or nature does not immediately entail unity in that which has the essence or nature, and plurality in essences or natures does not immediately imply plurality in that which has the essences or natures. This principle, as has already been shown, is of importance for the doctrine of the Trinity, and on the basis of what has just been said, it appears to be so for the doctrine of the person of Christ. The Thomist definition of a person, and that of Boethius, have already been cited.[38] It is worth noting that, according to these definitions, a

[34] They have been out of favour since the Second Vatican Council. This does not immediately entail that they are of no real significance.

[35] See p. 83 above.

[36] Lonergan's discussion is very abstract, and goes deep into traditional metaphysics. I have done my best to reproduce the gist.

[37] See pp. 90–91 above.

[38] See p. 92 above.

person is not said to *be* a rational or intellectual nature, but to be *in* or *of* it—in other words, a person *is* not an essence or nature, but *has* an essence or nature (Lonergan 1964c, 218, 221–22).

It may easily be seen how the metaphysical distinctions just drawn may be applied to the problem under discussion. Although the direct application of metaphysical distinctions is to the world of our experience, they may also be used to elucidate the revealed mysteries, or anything else which can meaningfully be said to exist or to occur. In the case of Christ, the one "person" is *that which is*, the subsistent being, Christ himself. The "natures" are those properties *by* which, or in virtue of which, he is on the one hand the eternal Word of God and on the other hand a man of a particular place and time. (Cases which present some sort of parallel are not far to seek. It is one thing to be the Prime Minister of Britain in 1982 and it is another to be the very famous woman called Margaret Thatcher. Yet the Prime Minister of Great Britain in 1982 and the very famous woman called Margaret Thatcher are one and the same.) Unity, as has been said, is what is known so far as it is judged on sufficient reason that A is B, but that it is not C, where "A," "B" and "C" all name subsistent beings. The sources of revelation provide sufficient reason for affirming that there is an eternal Word of God, that there was a man, Jesus, and that, while it is one thing *to be* the eternal Word of God and another thing *to be* the man Jesus (the "natures" or "essences" are distinct), the two are, at the level of "subsistent being," not distinct but one and the same (Lonergan 1964c, 231; 1956, 127).

Lonergan reviews a number of unsuccessful solutions to the problem just discussed. Duns Scotus and the Scotists held that to be a person is to be a subsistent being *without* certain properties and relations, for instance, that of real dependence on another such being. Because what was assumed, Christ's humanity, *had* such a real dependence on the divine Person who is the eternal Word, it did not itself amount to a person. Lonergan identifies the inadequacy of such a view. If a given entity *without* such dependence is a person, then the same entity *with* such dependence is just a dependent person. Scotus is really committed to the heretical thesis which he verbally denies, that it was a person which was assumed. The account given by Tiphanus is much the same as that of Scotus, despite the fact that it is expressed in a different way. A person, as he sees it, is the complete reality of a subsistent being, whole in itself, and such as cannot form a part or aspect of another whole. But Lonergan complains that what is involved here is merely the same entity conceived in different ways, as not part of a greater whole and as part of it. If in the former case we have a person, in the latter case we have a person included within a greater whole. Thus heretical conclusions are once again logically inevitable (Lonergan 1964c, 232; 1956, 34).

These mistaken accounts illustrate the fact that, short of an adequate theory of knowledge, systematic Christology is bound, as Lonergan expresses it, to be "bogged down in a precritical morass" (Lonergan, 1974, 25).

On the correct account, which in fact was provided by Aquinas,[39] what is constituted by the body and soul of the man Jesus is not *that which is*, a subsistent being or being in the primary sense. It is rather *that by which* something is, a being in the secondary sense. That which is, the person, is not so much the body together with the soul, as *the one who has* the body and soul. The body and soul do not fully constitute *that which is* a human being, the human being's self, but rather *that by which* one is a man, one's humanity. To put it in more modern terms, it is not just the embodied consciousness, it is the *subject of* that embodied consciousness. If this is so, it is conceivable that the subject of an embodied human consciousness might also be the subject of another kind of consciousness, which, in the case of the incarnate Word of God, could not be other than a divine consciousness (Lonergan 1964c, 231; 1956, 127).[40]

Someone might object that the kind of systematic Christology that Lonergan proposes was all very well before the rise of modern biblical criticism, but has now been rendered invalid by its methods and results. Lonergan admits the vital importance of biblical criticism for theology. It is indeed a corollary of his often-stated conviction that the Church has to come to terms with the scholarly differentiation of consciousness which first arose in the nineteenth century. The New Testament, as he says, does not immediately provide data about the historical Jesus himself, but about the beliefs of the communities within which its books were written. The truth about Jesus can only be determined, and then very tentatively, by historical inquiry. Fundamentalists regard every doubt of the *prima facie* implications of any statement by a New Testament writer as tantamount to a rejection of Christian faith, while secularists find a great deal in the New Testament to excite their incredulity. But Lonergan suggests that a mediating position may be arrived at, if religious persons can be induced to give up their pre-critical notions of history, and if learned persons can be brought to recognize in the New Testament contemporary and so first-hand evidence about the beliefs of the early Christian community.[41] At this rate, one might well at once be an orthodox Christian, who accepts the conciliar teachings as accurate determinations of the meaning of the true revelation of God in Jesus Christ, and a scientific historian who inquires with the utmost objectivity and rigor how the Jesus of history is likely to have acted, spoken, and thought.[42]

---

[39] *Summa Theologica*, III, xvii, 2.

[40] Lonergan 1964c, 231; 1956, 127: "Distinguendae sunt conscientiae quibus Christus est conscius, sed dividendum non est subjectum quod est conscium." For a discussion of the person of Christ, in relation to his two natures and two modes of consciousness, cf. Lonergan 1967, 164–97.

[41] Lonergan 1976, 56.

[42] My own view of this matter, which seems to be more or less implicit in what Lonergan says, is that while there is a sense in which rigorous historical investigation *might* tend to show that the words and deeds of the historical Jesus were quite incompatible with his being what

But the assured or likely consequences of contemporary scholarship are one thing, the results of inadequate conceptuality or sheer philosophical muddle quite another. Contemporary theology is very apt to resent any intrusion from philosophy, but, as Lonergan says, the result of this resentment is too frequently that it is unconsciously dominated by bad philosophy. In insisting that Jesus is a human person, contemporary theologians may fancy that they come into conflict with the traditional teachings of the Church. But the crucial question is whether the assertion that Jesus is a human person means "not simply that Jesus was a person and a man but effectively that Jesus was a person and a man and only a man. If it does not mean 'only a man,' then there is no conflict with faith in the pre-existent divine person who became a man. And if it does mean 'only a man,' then its source is not Christian preaching but Ebionite heresy" (Lonergan 1976b, 65). Lonergan does not feel that those theologians who express discontent with the traditional teaching have always confronted this dilemma in a clear-sighted way.[43]

---

traditional Christendom believes him to be, in fact it *will not* if Christianity is true. It is notable that Lonergan speaks with apparent agreement of those "moderate conservatives" among New Testament scholars who argue among themselves about whether a Christology was implicit or explicit in the words and deeds of the historical Jesus (Lonergan 1976, 51–52). Presumably, traditional Christianity would be falsified if it could be established beyond reasonable doubt that a Christology was not even implicit; then, "the factual presuppositions of the Christ of faith" (Lonergan 1976, 55) would be found not to obtain. However, it must be admitted that Lonergan does not emphasise that Christian faith might conceivably be falsified to the degree that at least one of his disciples would like him to have done. Cf. Lonergan 1985, 74–99.

[43] The work which Lonergan has particularly in mind is Schoonenberg 1971. On the relation of traditional Christology to the so-called 'new quest of the historical Jesus', and the curious claim that we can have no knowledge of his consciousness, see Meynell 1983. For a superb account of the intentions and motives of Jesus so far as these are recoverable to us, see Meyer 1979.

# Chapter 9

# THE WORK OF CHRIST

One might well argue that inadequate understanding has done more harm in the case of the doctrine of the atonement than in that of any other Christian doctrine. Very many who have impugned it have in fact, as Lonergan shows at length, had in mind not the doctrine itself, but a facile and inadequate interpretation of it. Here as elsewhere, those theologians who content themselves with such interpretations provide more reasons or pretexts for those disposed to reject Christian or Catholic doctrine. Historically speaking, it can be shown how Lutheran accounts of the atonement were rooted in a decadent scholasticism, and the denials of the doctrine by Socinians and rationalists can be understood largely as a reaction against these opinions of the Lutherans (Lonergan 1964c, 448).

Peter Abelard was condemned by the Catholic Church for denying that Christ took flesh in order to deliver us from the yoke of the devil,[1] and for saying that we did not contract fault as well as penalty from Adam.[2] He was later championed by liberal Protestant theologians as a precursor of their "moral influence" or "subjective" theory of the atonement, which again can be seen as a reaction against the classical Protestant account. Abelard taught that Christ redeemed us by showing forth the divine love, as a result of which we in our turn were excited to love and thus to obtain remission of our sins. "Our redemption," he wrote, "is that supreme love which is within us on account of the passion of Christ, which not only frees us from the slavery of sin, but gains for us the true freedom of the sons of God, so that we fulfill everything out of love for him rather than fear."[3] This grave oversimplification may be to some extent understood when one remembers that, in Abelard's time, the distinction between the methods proper to philosophy and to theology, which was one of the great intellectual achievements of the thirteenth century, had not yet been worked out (Lonergan 1964c, 450).

Lonergan says that when one examines biblical teaching on this matter, one should bear in mind the principle that God in his omnipotence rules and governs everything through secondary causes, that is to say, in accordance with scientific and historical laws. The factors which led to the death of Jesus

---

[1] DS 721, 723.

[2] DS 728.

[3] Abelard, *Expositio in epist. ad Romanos*, lib. II, ML 178, 833–836, esp. 836B.

as a matter of historical fact are brought out particularly by the Gospel of John, which not only describes the continuous opposition to Jesus, but draws attention to those factors which made this opposition more or less inevitable in the light of the usual course of human affairs. Jesus was the Word of God and the light of the world,[4] who had come into the world for the very purpose of bearing witness to the truth.[5] John the Baptist, the Scriptures, and God the Father himself corroborated his status and his mission.[6] But human beings loved darkness more than light, because their deeds were evil.[7] They acted blindly, but this was no excuse, since their blindness arose through hatred and so by their own fault (Lonergan 1964c, 453).[8]

One should also bear in mind the principles outlined by Aquinas on the relation of physical and moral evil to the purposes of God. God directly wills what is good, and indirectly wills the natural defect and the natural penalty for fault which are part and parcel of the order of the universe.[9] The evil of moral fault God does not will either directly or indirectly, but permits.[10] (In the case of the failures to decide well which are essentially constitutive of moral fault, it is better that there should be free moral agents than that there should not be, and that these should be allowed to fall away from goodness if they choose.) God "neither wills them to happen nor wills them not to happen, but wills to permit them to happen. And this is good."[11] Lonergan points out that both sorts of evil—what God indirectly wills and what God permits, as well as the good which God directly wills—can be clearly discerned in the passion of Christ. First, God did not in any way will, but merely permitted, the evil of fault, or the inner consent of the will to do wrong, in Judas, the chief priest, the crowd, the soldiers, and the others who were responsible for the death of Jesus. Second, God indirectly willed what ensued from the occurrence of these basic moral faults within the general order of the universe, that is to say, the overt actions of those who afflicted Jesus.[12] Third, God directly willed the obedience and love displayed by Christ himself (Lonergan 1964c, 455).

One may say that the evil of moral fault, which God in no way wills, is alluded to in the text, "This is your hour, and the power of darkness."[13] To say that God did not spare God's own Son[14] is as much as to say that God

---

[4] John 1:9.
[5] John 18:37.
[6] John 5:36–47.
[7] John 3:19–21, 7:7.
[8] John 15:24–25.
[9] *Summa Theologica*, I, ciii 2; xlvii 1; xciii 2.
[10] Ibid., I, xxiii 3.
[11] Ibid., I, xix 9.
[12] On God's permission of the evil of moral fault, see Lonergan 1971, 109–15; 1957, 666–68. Cf. Meynell 1976a, 136–38.
[13] Luke 22:53.
[14] Rom. 8:32.

indirectly willed the human actions which led to the suffering of Jesus. That God directly willed the obedience and love displayed by Jesus may be inferred both from the particular instance of the Father's command to the Son,[15] and from the general teaching of the New Testament, which repudiates the *lex talionis*, the principle of tit for tat, and commands the love of one's enemies.[16] Indeed, it commends explicitly the suffering of evil for righteousness' sake,[17] and it sets forth the sufferings of Jesus himself— unjustly inflicted yet patiently borne—as an example for us to follow.[18] And these three elements clearly contribute to a unity, both in general and in the particular case of our redemption. The sin of those who afflicted Christ, the suffering endured by Christ, and the love and patience displayed by Christ provide an instance of the good permission of God, the good indirect will of God, and the good direct will of God. All contribute to the same good effect, the redemption of humankind (Lonergan 1964c, 455–56).

What is to be understood by the notion of "redemption"? Where the Latin Vulgate has *redimere* and its cognates, which are the direct equivalents of the English "redeem," "redeemer," and "redemption," the Greek of the New Testament has a fairly wide range of expressions: *lutrousthai*,[19] *lutrōtes*,[20] *lutron*,[21] *antilutron*,[22] *lutrōsis*,[23] and *apolutrōsis*. These will be found, if one compares the Greek version of the Old Testament, to be equivalent to three verbs together with their cognate nouns in the Hebrew Old Testament: *Padah, pidyōn; Ga'al, ge'ūllah; Kipper, Kōfer. Padah,* "redeem," is used in the context of the deliverance of the Israelites from Egypt.[24] *Ga'al,* "liberate," seems to be used primarily in connection with the end of the Babylonian captivity, though it is applied to the exodus from Egypt as well.[25] *Kipper,* "expiate," is used of the removal of disease or sin, and is thus the vehicle for a profounder meaning for which these political liberations provide analogies. The cognate nouns are used of the means by which liberation or redemption is effected. A number of passages in the Old Testament explore the theme of deliverance from sin. The authors extol the holiness of God,[26] lament human offenses against God,[27] and celebrate the

---

[15] Cf. John 5:30.
[16] Matt. 5:38–48.
[17] Matt. 5:10–12.
[18] 1 Peter 2:19–24.
[19] Luke 24:21, Tit. 2:14.
[20] Acts 7:35.
[21] Mark 10:45, Matt. 20:28.
[22] 1 Tim. 2:6.
[23] Luke 1:68, 2:28; Heb. 9:12.
[24] Deut. 7:8, 9:26, 15:15, 24:18; cf. Acts 7:25.
[25] Jer. 31:7–11, Isa. 43; cf. Pss. 74:2, 77:16, 78:35.
[26] Isa. 6:1–5.
[27] Pss. 51:6.

redemption wrought by God.[28] Also, there is promise of a new covenant,[29] and mysterious mention of a suffering servant of God.[30]

To say that Christ effects the "redemption" of humanity is to see his work on the analogy of a commercial transaction. That the term is not to be understood literally is obvious enough, and in any case is implied by the statement of Scripture to the effect that the price is not paid in gold or silver.[31] But what is it that is expressed by the analogy? At the very least, it must imply a connection of some kind between something done and something else which is achieved by the doing of it. However stupid one is, and however ignorant one may be of the principles of science or metaphysics, at least one will be capable of understanding the basic principle of commercial transactions—if you want the goods, you must pay the price. Applied to the work of Christ, the analogy expresses the fact that the salvation of humanity was not to be had for nothing; Christ had to give up his life. This sense, as Lonergan says, is of course minimal; it can be and has been developed in a number of ways. Thus Christ's work has been understood in terms of some kind of substitution, death being the penalty of sin, such that Christ had to undergo death in the place of sinners. Alternatively, it may be conceived as the paying of a price *to* someone. Thus the Fathers will have it that the price is to be paid to the devil; the medieval theologians and their successors, that it is paid to God. Lonergan points out that the Fathers and the later theologians are not really contradicting one another, but talking about different aspects of the matter. What is "paid" to God is the sacrifice offered to God, that is, the passion and death of Christ as voluntarily undergone. What is "paid" to the devil is what is conceded to the powers of darkness, in the manner described above[32]—that is to say, the evil of fault which God does not will at all, and the consequent evil of Christ's afflictions which God wills only indirectly (Lonergan 1964c, 465–67).

The mission of the Son by the Father for the salvation of humanity is a matter both of the eternal procession of the Son and of his actions as a man; this may be inferred from what has been said already about the divine missions.[33] It is the actions of the Son as man which involve that kind of relation to the behest of another which may properly be termed "obedience."[34] To command someone, as Aquinas says, is to influence him by way of his reason and will,[35] and, conversely, to obey is to be influenced through one's reason and will by another.[36] (I cannot strictly speaking, as a

---

[28] Isa. 40:1–5; 43:1, 3–4; 44:22; 45:2, 4; etc.

[29] Isa. 55:3–8; Jer. 31:31–34.

[30] Isa. 42:1–7, 49:1–6, 50:4–9, 52:13, 53:12; Ps. 22.

[31] 1 Pet. 1:18.

[32] Cf. Luke 12:53, Heb. 2:14, 15.

[33] See pp. 97–101 above.

[34] Cf. Heb. 5:8.

[35] *Summa Theologica*, II-II, civ 1.

[36] Ibid., III, xlvii 2.

matter of logic, obey anyone, unless I understand what he is telling me to do, and consent to act accordingly.) Lonergan considers the argument that Christ cannot be claimed in any sense to be "obedient," given that sin was no real option for him, and that any lack of conformity on his part with the Father's will would have been sinful. Now in our fallen nature, it is obvious enough that the spirit may be willing and the flesh weak, and that there may in consequence be a great deal of difference between merely wanting to do something and actually carrying it through. This discrepancy, though it certainly seems increased by our state of sin, does seem to have some foundation in the difference between our intellectual and rational nature on the one hand and our sensitive nature on the other. This difference is natural to us quite apart from sin. Thus while our intellectual and rational nature is orientated towards knowing what is true and knowing and doing what is good, our sensitive nature is inclined to follow whatever appeals to our senses and to the appetites which go with them.

Although he was sinless, Christ as man would often have had to go against his feelings and desires in order to do what he had to do, and it is in this subjection of his sensitive nature that his obedience may be said to have consisted (Lonergan 1964c, 475–77). Thus we may understand how the Word made flesh[37] so became embodied, so shared our human flesh and blood,[38] that he became like us his sisters and brothers in all things,[39] and in accordance with this was tested in every way, yet without sin.[40] Since his supreme work of love[41] was to be carried through to such a pitch of bodily suffering, it is no wonder that the Gospels tell us of his strength of feeling,[42] the turmoil of his mind,[43] his fear, his weariness, and his overwhelming grief.[44] It may indeed be said that Christ was perfected through his sufferings,[45] learned obedience through what he endured,[46] not as though to imply that he advanced in moral goodness as such, but because he came in time to perform actions which exemplified this goodness in the highest degree (Lonergan 1964c, 475–77).

Christ's satisfaction consists in his vicarious suffering and death on account of sins and on behalf of sinners. But to set down the mere fact is one thing, to understand it another. An understanding of the matter presupposes some grasp of the nature of sin, of the penalties for sins, and of the nature of divine justice. There are two sorts of circumstances, according to Lonergan,

37 John 1:14.
38 Heb. 10:5.
39 Heb. 2:14.
40 Heb. 2:17.
41 Heb. 4:15.
42 John 15:13.
43 Luke 12:50.
44 Mark 15:34.
45 Heb. 2:10.
46 Heb. 5:5.

in which "satisfaction" may be given for offences. The first are those in which there is no question of forgiveness being either asked for or conceded; the only kind of justice at issue here is that which may be termed "retributive." The second are those in which the main emphasis is on the expression of detestation for and sorrow at the offence, on forgiveness asked for and granted, and on remission both of the blame and of the punishment which accrues to it. Now it is of the utmost importance for this whole question, as Lonergan sees it, to grasp that any "penalties" paid by Christ, and any "satisfaction" which he may give, must be of this second type. They cannot be of the first, since, given that he has done no wrong, he cannot be punished retributively. Whether satisfaction is given in the first type of way (by the punishment of sinful human beings), or the second (by Christ's atoning work), the effect is that the order of divine justice, which has been damaged by sin, is repaired and re-integrated. There is no third way. Satisfaction must be given, either of the first type or of the second. All this seems simple and obvious enough, but neglect of its implications has led to an enormous amount of misunderstanding (Lonergan 1964c, 488–90).

Lonergan explains that Christ's satisfaction for sin is to be conceived on the analogy of the expression of an attitude by one human person to what has happened or been done to another. For example, if Smith has been deeply offended, Jones can say, "Fine! He got what he deserved." At that rate the offence against Smith has certainly not been removed. But Jones may be indignant at the offence, may vehemently maintain the injustice of it, and may show by every means at his disposal that he takes the part of the offended party. In this way, the offence is diminished, and some kind of compensation is made for it. It is on this model that we may obtain some kind of understanding of the satisfaction wrought by Christ for the offence against God constituted by sin. If Christians have "not yet considered how great is the gravity of sin," as Anselm puts it,[47] meditation on the Lord's passion certainly brings it home to them. The seriousness of the offence against God must indeed be great, if it was appropriate for Christ to suffer so much, and if no other reason can be given for that suffering except satisfaction for sin. In light of what has just been said, one can understand the remark of Aquinas, "He properly gives satisfaction for an offence who shows to him who has been offended something which he loves as much as or more than he hates the offence",[48] or that of Anselm, "This life" [that of Christ] "is more lovable than sins are hateful."[49]

It is not necessarily wrong to think of the suffering and death of Christ as "penalties." What is crucial is not to misunderstand the concept of "penalty" as used in this context. Christ gave satisfaction so that our sins might be

[47] Anselm, *Cur Deus homo*, I, 21.
[48] *Summa Theologica*, III, xlviii, 2.
[49] Anselm, *Cur Deus homo*, ii, 14. DVI 537.[50] *Summa Theologica*, III, xiv, 1, 3, 4.

forgiven. He did this by expressing horror and detestation of the offence against God involved, and he underwent intense suffering and death as a means of doing so. Only in this sense did he pay a "penalty." Aquinas states it this way: while Our Lord's sufferings were the "matter" of the satisfaction that he gave, its "principle" was his charity.[50] (He gave satisfaction, as one might put it, *by* expressing and embodying detestation of the offence against God involved in sin, and the *means* by which he did this was his suffering and death.) However, not everyone has the wisdom of Aquinas, and one may gain some understanding of conflicting opinions on this matter by seeing them in the light of his conception of it (Lonergan 1964c, 492–93).

Some theological views of the matter are deficient only in that an adequate systematic context for the notion of "satisfaction" had not yet evolved when they were proposed. Lonergan distinguishes two principal stages in the development of this systematic context, that up to Anselm and that from Anselm to Aquinas' *Summa Theologica*. Anselm concentrated particularly on that aspect of the atonement which consists in compensation for the offence against God; Aquinas integrated this understanding of the mystery with the traditional doctrine of the penalties incurred by Christ. Other views fall short because they develop Anselm's account in terms of a viewpoint which is systematic but defective. This is illustrated by Duns Scotus, who deals with the satisfaction wrought by Christ in much the same way as he deals with other problems in theology. That is, he sets out to prove that this or that is absolutely possible, and that the other is absolutely necessary, and so overlooks the understanding of things which is actually to be had. Finally, he falls back on some kind of voluntarism; what is so is so just because God willed it, and that is that. Other illustrations are provided by those attempted solutions which appeal to some kind of hypothetical juridical contract; for example, that Christ at once *ought* to have died, and *freely accepted* his death, is explained on the hypothesis that Christ freely entered into a contract which he was subsequently obliged to honor (Lonergan 1964c, 493).

A third way of falling short in attempting to understand the atonement is to pervert the notion of "satisfaction." Thus the suffering by Christ of pains which ought to have been suffered by us is taken to be the principal element in it. Christ gives satisfaction for our sins because he suffers enough for them, and the point of his sufferings as expressing horror at sin and the affront offered by it to God falls out of the picture. And this account more or less inevitably leads to the doctrine of substitution, whereby Christ takes the place of sinners in the sense that he suffers or is punished enough for God justly to forgive other humans and remit their penalties. Such conceptions are typical of the older Protestant authors, but not only of them. They are found also in Catholic preachers or controversialists, who thought them well adapted to their purposes, and even in some systematic theologians, who appeared to think that such an account was nothing other than the genuinely Catholic one (Lonergan 1964c, 494).

In order to clarify further the point at issue, it is worth bearing in mind the difference between the realm of common-sense and that of theory which has already been alluded to a number of times in this book. The common-sense mentality does not operate with precisely-defined concepts; it uses rhetorical devices of persuasion rather than rigorous proofs, and is inclined to express much by means of a single image or set of images rather than taking each topic separately and in order. There is nothing wrong, far from it, with the common-sense mentality in itself; it is present in the most cultivated persons as well as among the uneducated. What leads to trouble is when a way of talking which is quite proper in a common-sense context becomes understood as though in a systematic one. This is very well illustrated by theories of the atonement (Lonergan 1964c, 534–35).

Among the older Protestant authors, Calvin held that God in his justice does not confer grace unless his anger is placated by expiation. For this Christ's mere death was insufficient; he had to undergo the pains of hell as well (cf. Franks 1918, 1:427–28, 431, 434). Calvin provides the historical context for Socinus' denial of the doctrine of Christ's satisfaction—that is to say, it was Calvin's exposition of the doctrine which Socinus repudiated in the first instance (Lonergan 1964c, 495–96). The theory which became generally accepted among the Lutherans was that of Quenstedt. He held that God, on account of his justice, cannot but demand the payment of the whole debt for sin. Without such payment, God absolutely cannot remit sins. Christ gave satisfaction both for all sins and for all the penalties accruing to them, and did this by voluntarily taking the whole of our debt upon himself, meeting the demands of justice fully by actually undergoing the pains of hell (Franks 1918, 2:81–83). Of the many Catholic preachers and controversialists who have defended a virtually Protestant theory of satisfaction, the name of Bossuet is perhaps the best known (Lonergan 1964c, 496–96b).

The later scholastic theologians, from the sixteenth to the nineteenth centuries, have not received much attention from recent investigators. J. Rivière remarks curtly that the prolixity of their controversies on this matter is out of proportion to their importance.[51] However, the many studies undertaken by Rivière himself have awakened interest once again in the question among Catholic theologians. Two points in particular seem to have emerged as requiring clarification. The first is the question of how God could directly will the satisfaction wrought by Christ, given that God does not directly will the evil of punishment.[52] The second is the question of whether Christ took upon himself not only our punishment but also, in some way, our

---

[51] "De ces longues controverses, l'importance n'égale pas l'ampleur" Rivière 1930, 1951).

[52] *Summa Theologica*, I, xix 9; Rivière 1930, 1973.

blame, so that it can really and truly be said that he suffered through God's retributive justice (Lonergan 1964c, 495, 496c).

Lonergan's answer to the first question is that what the Father directly willed was not Christ's sufferings as such, but his endurance and patient acceptance of them through obedience and love. As for the second question, Lonergan notes that whether terms like "punishment" and "penalty" are applied to the sufferings of Christ is not in itself of much importance. The serious question is whether it was on account of God's retributive justice that Christ suffered for us and for our sins. What is of crucial importance is that Christ *took upon himself* his sufferings; he did not in any sense *owe* them. He could only have owed them only if he had been guilty himself, as no Christian could possibly admit, or if, as on some classical Protestant views, he had somehow had the guilt of sin transferred or imputed to him. But the mere existence of offence is not enough for the exercise of retributive justice, except when this is inflicted on the one who is guilty of the offence. To claim otherwise is to have a conception of retributive justice which is either immoral or amoral. It is no wonder that the doctrine of the redemption is itself rejected, when it is assumed to have such implications (Lonergan 1964c, 497).

Anselm's fundamental point is this. Once God's honor is impugned, it is necessary either that punishment should follow or that it should be vindicated in some other way. Otherwise, God is either unjust to self or impotent in respect to creation, neither of which conclusions are acceptable.[53] This disjunction, either satisfaction or punishment, is at the basis of Anselm's theory of the atonement, which may be summarised as follows. Mere humanity in any case owes everything to God, and so is constitutionally incapable of making amends for wrongs done to God.[54] However, the God-man is under no obligation, and hence can give the required satisfaction, over and above what is owed, by dying.[55] The satisfaction wrought by the God-man outweighs all sins, and merits their remission (Lonergan 1964c, 498).[56]

In connection with this argument of Anselm's, it is worth noting that the distinction between the methods proper to philosophy and to theology had not yet been evolved. The incompleteness in his argument which is due to this comes out when one asks whether the disjunction, either satisfaction or punishment, really exhausts the possibilities. To cope with this question, one must distinguish between the actual scheme of things and other possible schemes. Given the actual scheme of things, in which God has acted to remedy the havoc wrought by human sin in the manner in which it is

[53] Anselm, *Cur Deus homo*, I, 13.
[54] Ibid., I, 19–24.
[55] Ibid., II, 11.
[56] Ibid., II, 14–15, 19.

revealed to us that God has (an assumption accepted by the Christian theologian), the disjunction is indeed exhaustive; given some other intrinsically possible schemes (such as the philosopher may envisage), it would not have been so. That God *might* otherwise have saved us from our sins is the general opinion among Catholic theologians; the fact remains that God *has* not done so.[57] From the perspective of later Catholic theology, which teaches that the incarnation and death of the Son were, strictly speaking, *appropriate* rather than *absolutely necessary* means to the salvation of humanity, Anselm's insistence that Christ's incarnation and death were absolutely necessary is a weakness in his account (Lonergan 1964c, 500–1).

Lonergan considers whether "giving satisfaction" and "paying the penalty" really amount to the same thing in this context, and whether the disjunction, "either satisfaction or penalty," means anything other than that punishment is undergone either by Christ or by the rest of us in hell. The older Protestant theologians, as has already been said, held that giving satisfaction and paying the penalty in effect amounted to the same thing. Catholic theologians have disagreed among themselves, some coming close to the Protestant position, others keeping their distance from it. But the controversy on this topic has been vitiated by lack of exact definitions of "satisfaction" and "penalty," and consequent lack of a clear distinction between the one and the other.

There seem to be two groups of mutually related concepts. The one involves fault, guilt, and the exacting of condign penalty; the other, satisfaction, the asking for and conceding of pardon, and remission of the penalty. Although these two groups are strictly speaking distinct from one another, they are very much mixed up with one another in their application to complex human affairs and as a consequence unless one sets oneself "piously, diligently and soberly" to understand the matter,[58] one will in no time be swamped in a morass of indistinct notions and ever more complex applications of them (Lonergan 1964c, 502–3).

"Pardon" means the remission of an offence when this is asked for and conceded; it is obviously to be contrasted with punishment justly inflicted.[59] "Satisfaction" is the voluntary undergoing of pain in order that pardon may appropriately be asked for and granted. Conceptually speaking, there is quite clearly a world of difference between voluntary acceptance of punishment on the one hand and the utterly enforced infliction of it on the other. In human affairs, of course, there are all manner of gradations between these two extremes. Pardon is "appropriate" when it is intelligible as part of a wise and prudent ordering of things; it does not have to be absolutely necessary, nor merely logically possible and free from contradiction. Examples of this

---

[57] For the distinction between philosophical and theological method as it developed historically, see Lonergan 1971, 13–19.

[58] DS 3016.

[59] Cf. Matt. 5:23–26; 6:12, 14, 15; 18:21–35; Mark 11:25–26; Luke 7:47; 17:3–4.

sort of intelligibility are to be found in the natural sciences, as well as in the supernatural order in which Christians share through faith in Jesus Christ. One discovers a certain intelligibility in things which absolutely speaking *could* have been otherwise, but as a matter of fact *are* as we find them to be through inquiry into the relevant range of data.[60]

In what sense, if any, is the satisfaction wrought by Christ for human sin "vicarious"? Satisfaction is vicarious so far as the offence in regard to which one acts is other than one's own. Lonergan mentions the objection that although "vicarious satisfaction" is evidence enough of the good will of the one that offers it, it does nothing to show the good will of the offender, and hence cannot remove the offence. But, following Aquinas, he notes that to make this objection is to overlook what lies at the basis of the possibility of vicarious satisfaction, the union of wills in love.[61] For if my friend suffers for me, it is as though I suffered myself. I suffer myself in sympathy with my friend, the more so, when I am the cause of that friend's suffering. And the love of one who suffers for another, because of the greatness of the love which is expressed in this way, is more acceptable to God than is suffering for one's own offence.[62] In the order of natural love and affection, love between an offender and one who gives satisfaction for the offence not only founds but also precedes the giving of satisfaction. But in the supernatural order, the love shown by Christ in giving satisfaction comes to evoke love in the offender where it had not previously existed (Lonergan 1964c, 510–12).

The divine order, which is broken by the offence of sin, is restored either by the punishment of the offender or by a giving of satisfaction for the offence. Those whose head is the devil merely undergo inflicted penalties for their offences. But the debt of those whose head is Christ is paid in another way, through the vicarious satisfaction which takes place through the love which it evokes. The more vehement the love of human persons for God, and the more intense their regret for their past faults, the more they are confirmed in good, and the less punishment is due to them. This remark is not to be understood in Pelagian terms,[63] as though sinners in and of themselves were able to display such love and compunction. What is at issue is a supernatural love which is not to be found except in Christ and through Christ.[64] For Christ is head of his body which is the Church; he gave himself for it, to make it holy,[65] giving satisfaction for his members to whom he is united in love.[66]

---

[60] Lonergan 1964c, 508–509.

[61] *Summa Theologica*, I–II, xxviii, 1 and 2.

[62] *Summa contra Gentes*, III, 158, 7. Aquinas cites Gal. 6:2.

[63] Pelagianism is the theological view that human beings take the first and crucial steps to salvation by their own efforts without divine grace. See Lonergan 1971, 2, 6, 48 *et passim*.

[64] This does not immediately imply that the grace bestowed in and through Christ is not at work in some who are not professing Christians, and in other religious traditions. See Lonergan 1972, 108–109. Cf. also Lonergan 1985, 55–73.

[65] Eph. 5: 2.

[66] *Summa Theologica*, III, xlviii, 2.

Thus the order of divine justice is restored, and out of the direst evils is brought forth that great good which is the body of Christ—the militant, suffering, and triumphant Church (Lonergan 1964c, 518–19).

There is a *prima facie* difficulty in reconciling Anselm's account of the atonement with that which had already become traditional by his time. Anselm distinguished satisfaction and penalty, and said that Christ had given satisfaction but not paid a penalty. However, the tradition maintained that Christ paid a penalty, and Anselm's authority was not sufficient to oust this way of speaking. After all, according to Scripture, death is the penalty for sin.[67] But Christ underwent death, and it is therefore only natural to infer that he paid the penalty for sin. Thus Augustine says of Christ, "Taking the penalty upon him, but not the fault, he destroyed both fault and penalty."[68] Peter Lombard maintained that Christ took upon himself not our fault, but our infirmities, and so the penalty of our sin; he passed over Anselm's opinion in silence. Alexander of Hales tried to tackle the problem by distinguishing various senses of the word "penalty" (Lonergan 1964c, 520–22).

Given what has been said, it is clear enough that, on Lonergan's view, the difficulty of reconciling Anselm's opinion with the traditional one is merely verbal. (Jesus "paid the penalty" for sin, insofar as he gave vicarious satisfaction in the manner described; he did *not* do so, insofar as it is implied thereby that he was at fault, or that the fault was in some immoral or incomprehensible manner transferred to him.) Aquinas put the matter well when he said that Christ took upon himself the defects which were the penalties for sin, in order that they should provide the material basis for his satisfaction for human sin.[69] The point to be noted here is the distinction, already mentioned as that made by Aquinas, between the material basis (*materia*) for the satisfaction and the principle (*principium*) which at once motivates the satisfaction and constitutes it as such. The material basis is the "penalty" not contracted through sin but freely taken up; the principle is charity or supernatural love.[70] (The satisfaction wrought by Christ consists in the expression of his love, and of the detestation of the offence against God involved in sin. The *means* by which he expresses this are his sufferings and death.) Although Christ, who was without fault, could have taken upon himself human nature without the penalty accruing to human fault, he took the "penalty" upon himself in order to achieve the work of our redemption.[71] Aquinas conceives "satisfaction" basically in the same manner as Anselm, but goes far beyond him in explaining how Christ's satisfaction can be vicarious through the love between Christ the head and us the members of his body (Lonergan 1964c, 523–25).

Christ did not take man's fault upon himself, except in a rhetorical

---

[67] Gen. 2:17; Rom. 5:12, 6:23.
[68] *Sermon* 171, 3; ML 38, 934.
[69] *Summa Theologica*, III, xiv, 1, 3–4.
[70] Ibid., 1.
[71] Ibid., 3.

manner of speaking. That is, he did not himself have sin of any kind, or take upon himself the sin of others by having it "imputed" to him[72] or by some kind of judicial contract. How, then, can Christ give satisfaction for us if he does not somehow take our blame upon himself? The answer is that he is in a position to give satisfaction for all as the new Adam,[73] as the inaugurator of a new and better covenant,[74] and as the head of his body the Church to which all human beings are called.[75] This explanation seems solid and well-founded enough, and is not in the least improved by the postulation of some quasi-judicial contract. As Lonergan remarks, here as elsewhere it seems fruitless to multiply hypotheses which cannot possibly be verified. It may be asked whether Christ gave satisfaction only for the faithful. The answer is that he died for all human beings,[76] since everyone can and ought to become a member of his body the Church (Lonergan 1964c, 530–31).

One way of expressing the solution to these problems is to say that while Christ suffered in accordance with divine justice, he did not suffer in accordance with divine *retributive* justice. Unless one grasps this principle, one inevitably becomes entangled in that mass of errors and confusions which have obscured this question from the sixteenth century onwards. For the penalties which are due to divine retributive justice are the pains of hell. This was why Calvin, and others among the older Protestant authorities, concluded that Christ underwent the pains of hell.[77] Furthermore, as Lonergan remarks, it is evident enough that the penalties due to retributive justice are owed once and not twice. From this, it may easily be inferred that guilt is never remitted through the merits of Christ without all penalty being remitted as well, which conflicts with the Catholic doctrine of purgatory and with what was defined at the Council of Trent.[78] There is another heretical consequence as well, that Christ died for the elect and not for all humanity;[79] otherwise, the penalties of the reprobate would no longer be owing, having already been undergone by Christ. Although these overtly un-Catholic conclusions can be evaded by bad logic, such an evasion is hardly to be recommended unequivocally. Sure enough, it is a good thing to disagree with heretics. But logical incoherence at once obscures the meaning and implications of Catholic doctrine, and brings the faith into disrepute among unbelievers (Lonergan 1964c, 530–31).[80]

It is to be noted that Anselm did *not* teach that Christ paid the penalty

---

[72] This notion of the "imputation" of righteousness to those who were and remained sinners was developed by fifteenth-century scholastics, and was of central importance for the theology of Luther.

[73] 1 Cor. 15:45.

[74] Heb. 7:22.

[75] Eph. 1:22–23. *Summa Theologica*, III, xlviii, 2; xlix, 3.

[76] DS 2005.

[77] DS 1870.

[78] DS 1712.

[79] DS 2005–6.

[80] Cf. Rom. 2:24.

required by God's retributive justice. It is of the essence of his account that Christ's act was supererogatory, beyond and above what divine justice required, and thus such that only the God-man could offer it. To say that God the Son was scourged, crucified, and put to death because of God's retributive justice implies *either* that Christ was guilty or somehow took the guilt of others upon himself *or* that God's retributive justice responds to offences without regard to the guilt of the person or persons punished. The former supposition, as Lonergan points out, is heretical by Catholic standards, the latter, immoral or amoral, and implying a view of God which is more or less blasphemous (Lonergan 1964c, 534).

Human sin is such that sins generate corrupt situations, and corrupt situations incline to further sin, both in the lives of individuals and in the social order (Lonergan 1957, chaps. 7, 18, 20). God could have dealt with the resulting mass of evil by the sheer exercise of power, in the manner apparently expected by Jewish messianism at the beginning of the Christian era. But in fact God chose to deal with it by that just and mysterious "law of the cross" which transforms those very evils into that highest good which is the body of Christ, head and members, in this life and in the life to come. The Fathers thus praise the manner of our redemption as wrought by Jesus, who is meek and lowly of heart,[81] who came not to be served but to serve, and to give his life as a ransom for many.[82] They contrast it with the way of the devil and of human pride, whereby one's ends are to be gained by the acquisition and exercise of power.[83]

What may be called "the law of the cross" is the principle according to which evil is turned into good in the manner exemplified by the death of Christ. In accordance with this law Christians are to be conformed to the image of God's Son, to suffer with him so that they may be glorified with him.[84] Of course, one should never forget that the law of the cross applies in one way to Christ, and in quite another to his members. It is found in him as the cause of salvation to all who obey him.[85] It is found in his members as in those who receive salvation from him, not of course merely passively or inertly, but through their active cooperation, as persons who are to learn and to believe, to live and work in and through Christ, to be assimilated and conformed to him in his death and resurrection (Lonergan 1964c, 556–57).

The transformation of evil into good, of death into life, is expressed and enjoined in the New Testament in many ways. First, there is the sacramental way. We share in Christ's death in our baptism, and as he is risen we walk in newness of life.[86] Then there is the moral way. We are to think of ourselves as

[81] Matt. 11:29.
[82] Mark 10:45.
[83] Augustine, *De Trin.*, XIII, xiii, 17; ML 42, 1046–7. Rivière 1930, 1939–40 has a great deal more to the point.
[84] Rom. 8:29, 17.
[85] Heb. 5:9.
[86] Rom. 6:4; cf. Col. 2:12, 1 Cor. 11:26.

dead to sin, but alive to God in Christ our Lord,[87] and to live our lives accordingly. Third, there is the ascetical way. We die if we live according to the flesh, we live if we mortify the flesh.[88] Fourth, there is the eschatological way. Our conversation is in heaven, whence we await our Lord Jesus Christ, who will transform our vile bodies into the likeness of his glorious body.[89] It is commended to us in the form of love of our enemies,[90] of daily acceptance of our cross,[91] of losing our lives for the sake of Christ and the Gospel that we may find them, in the likeness of the seed that dies and brings forth fruit,[92] in expectation of the happiness promised to those who patiently endure suffering (Lonergan 1964c, 571).[93]

However, as Lonergan reminds us, the law of the cross, despite its sovereign efficacy in the realm of the spirit and its general applicability to human affairs, does not have the universality of a law of nature. It is thus not obviously right to the merely natural human intelligence, however acute. We are told, in fact, that the law of the cross is not acknowledged or accepted except through the gift of the Holy Spirit.[94] It is for this reason that there are many who are enemies of the cross of Christ—and not merely, in our own times, those whose god is their belly.[95] There are those who have deliberately and explicitly developed a philosophy in opposition to it. Thus Nietzsche stigmatized Christian forebearance and humility as the attitude of slaves, who, out of intense but repressed hatred for the virtues of their masters, choose to consider their own servile laziness as virtuous. And Marx ascribed Christian patience and long-suffering not to divine wisdom, but to an ideology fabricated by the rich, the more easily to enjoy the good things of the world by deceiving the poor with the vain hope of a future life. These errors of course are the more influential, the more evidently those who profess the name of Christ show that they care little for the law of Christian living (Lonergan 1964c, 574–75).

[87] Rom. 6:11, cf. Col. 3:1–4.
[88] Rom. 8:13; cf. 1 Cor. 9:27.
[89] Phil. 3:20–21.
[90] Matt. 5:43–48.
[91] Mark 8;34, Matt. 16:24, Luke 9:23.
[92] Mark 8:35, Matt. 16:28, Luke 9:24.
[93] Matt. 5:11–12.
[94] 1 Cor. 1:18–31, 2:10–16.
[95] Phil. 3:18–19.

# Chapter 10

# CONCLUSION

An anonymous British critic has seen fit to dismiss Lonergan's work as 'sheer pedantry'. How, if at all, could such a charge be answered?

The Catholic and Christian faith has been expressed in a wide range of ways against a bewildering variety of cultural and intellectual backgrounds. One may well wonder whether there is any underlying unity in this variety, and if so, whether there is any good reason for believing in it.

One might suppose that both of these questions were serious. It is indeed difficult to see what questions could be of greater significance, so long as Christianity or Catholicism are serious options at all. And Lonergan has confronted both questions head-on. Against a background of an investigation of human knowledge and of what is to be known by it, he advances reasons for belief in God, Christ, and (in rather less detail) the special office of the Church. He further shows how the central Christian doctrines of the Trinity, the Incarnation, and the Atonement are based on Scripture, how they are expounded and clarified ever more fully by the Church over the course of time, and how they are relevant to human life in all its boundless aspiration and tragic despair. In addition, Lonergan provides a method of inquiry by which in principle members of every religion and denomination may justify, clarify, and amplify the spiritual riches available within their own traditions.

# BIBLIOGRAPHY

Ayer, A. J., 1958. *Language, Truth and Logic*. London: Gollancz.

Barth, K., 1936–62. *Church Dogmatics*. Edinburgh: T. & T. Clark.

Collingwood, R. G., 1939. *An Autobiography*. London: Oxford University Press.

Corcoran, P. (ed.), 1975. *Looking at Lonergan's Method*. Dublin: Talbot Press.

Cullman, O., 1957., 1963. *Christologie des Neuen Testaments*. Tübingen: Mohr.

Denzinger, H. and Schönmetzer, A. (DS), 1963. *Enchiridion Symbolorum*. Barcelona: Herder.

Emmet, D. M., 1973. "The Double Conversion of Karl Rahner and Bernard Lonergan." *Theoria to Theory* 7, 12–20.

Evans, D., 1980. *Faith, Authenticity and Morality*. Toronto: Toronto University Press.

Franks, R. L., 1918. *The History of the Doctrine of the Work of Christ*. London: Hodder and Stoughton.

Freud, S., 1933. *Introductory Lectures on Psychoanalysis*. London: Allen and Unwin.

Galtier, P., 1939. *L'unité du Christ*. Paris: Beauchesne.

Galtier, P., 1947. *De Incarnatione*. Paris: Beauchesne.

Geach, P. and Black M., 1980. *Translations from the Writings of Gottlob Frege*. Oxford: Blackwell.

Gutwenger, E., 1960. *Bewusstsein und Wissen Christi*. Innsbruck: F. Rauch.

Hare, R. M., 1966. *The Language of Morals*. New York: Oxford University Press.

Hebblethwaite, B., 1980. *The Practice of Theology*. Cambridge: Cambridge University Press.

Heiler, F., 1959. "The History of Religions as the Preparation for the Cooperation of Religions." *The History of Religions*, ed. M. Eliade and J. Kitagawa. Chicago: Chicago University Press, 142–53.

Hepburn, R. W., 1973. "Method and Insight." *Philosophy* 48, 153–60.

Kuhn, T. S., 1962. *The Structure of Scientific Revolutions*. Chicago: Chicago University Press.

Lakatos, I. and Musgrave A. (eds.), 1970. *Criticism and the Growth of Knowledge*. Cambridge: Cambridge University Press.

Lampe, G. W. H., 1977. *God as Spirit*. Oxford: Clarendon Press.

Lonergan, B. J. F., 1956. *De Constitutione Christi*. Rome: Gregorian University Press.

Lonergan, B. J. F., 1957. *Insight. A Study of Human Understanding*. London: Longmans, Green and Co.

Lonergan, B. J. F., 1964a. *De Deo Trino. I. Pars Dogmatica*. Rome: Gregorian University Press.

Lonergan, B. J. F., 1964b. *De Deo Trino. II. Pars Systematica*. Rome: Gregorian University Press.

Lonergan, B. J. F., 1964c. *De Verbo Incarnato*. Rome: Gregorian University Press.

Lonergan, B. J. F., 1967. *Collection*. London: Darton, Longman and Todd.

Lonergan, B. J. F., 1968. *Verbum. Word and Idea in Aquinas*. London: Darton, Longman and Todd.

Lonergan, B. J. F., 1971. *Grace and Freedom*. London: Darton, Longman and Todd.

Lonergan, B. J. F., 1972. *Method in Theology*. London: Darton, Longman and Todd.

Lonergan, B. J. F., 1973a. *Philosophy of God and Theology*. London: Darton, Longman and Todd.

Lonergan, B. J. F., 1973b. "System, Common Sense, Scholarship." *Cultural Hermeneutics* I, 85–96.

Lonergan, B. J. F., 1974. *A Second Collection*. London: Darton, Longman and Todd.

Lonergan, B. J. F., 1976a. *The Way to Nicea*. London: Darton, Longman and Todd.

Lonergan, B. J. F., 1976. "Christology Today. Methodological Reflections." R. Laflamme and M. Gervais eds., *Le Christ hier, aujourd' hui et demain* (Québec: Les Presses de L'Université Laval), 45–65.

Lonergan, B. J. F., 1985. *A Third Collection*. New York: Paulist Press.

Manser, A., 1966. *Sartre. A Philosophical Study*. London: Athlone Press.

Meyer, B. F., 1979. *The Aims of Jesus*. London: SCM Press.

Meynell, H. A., 1973. "The Theology of Hartshorne." *Journal of Theological Studies* 24, 143–57.

Meynell, H. A., 1976a. *An Introduction to the Philosophy of Bernard Lonergan*. London: Macmillans.

Meynell, H. A., 1976b. "The Holy Trinity and the Corrupted Consciousness." *Theology* 79, 143–51.

Meynell, H. A., 1982. "Two Directions for Pneumatology." *Religious Studies Bulletin* 2, 101–16.

Meynell, H. A., 1983. "A Christological Jeremiad." *The Month* 245, 52–58.

Migne, J. P., 1857–66. *Patrologia Graeca* (MG). Paris: Lutetiae.

Migne, J. P., 1844–64. *Patrologia Latina* (ML). Paris: Lutetiae.

O'Donnell, J. J., 1982. "The Doctrine of the Trinity in Recent German Theology." *The Heythrop Journal* 23, 153–70.

Opitz, H. G., 1934. *Athanasius Werke*. Berlin & Leipzig: de Gruyter.

Peirce, C. S., 1958. *Values in a Universe of Chance*. Stanford: Stanford University Press.

Popper, K. R., 1972. *Objective Knowledge*. Oxford: Clarendon Press.

Prestige, G. L., 1936. *God in Patristic Thought*. London: SPCK.

Rahner, K., 1971. "Some Critical Thoughts on Functional Specialties in Theology." P. McShane ed. *Foundations of Theology*. Dublin: Gill & Macmillan, 194–96.

Rahner, K., 1978. *Foundations of Christian Faith*. London: Darton, Longman and Todd.

Reichmann, J. B., 1968. "The Transcendental Method and the Psychogenesis of Being." *The Thomist* 32, 449–508.

Rivière, J., 1930. "Rédemption." *Dictionnaire de Théologie Catholique*. Paris: Letousey et Ané, XIII, 1951–2004.

Schoonenberg, P., 1971. *The Christ*. New York: Seabury Press.

Shea, W. F., 1976. "The Stance and Task of the Foundational Theologian." *The Heythrop Journal* 17, 273–292.

Strawson, P. F., 1966. *The Bounds of Sense*. London: Methuen.

Tyrrell, B., 1974. *Bernard Lonergan's Philosophy of God*. Dublin: Gill and Macmillan.

Willer, J., 1972. *The Social Determination of Knowledge*. Princeton: Prentice Hall.

Winch, P., 1958. *The Idea of a Social Science*. London: Routledge and Kegan Paul.

Wittgenstein, L., 1953. *Philosophical Investigations*. Oxford: Blackwell.